Contents

Chapter 4. Comprehension: Active Thinking About the Text

HELPING STRUGGLING READERS

Successful Reading Techniques

Susan Fondrk
MS Education

Cheryl Frasca
MA Education

Mrs. I. Nand

Good Year Books
Parsippany, New Jersey

Good Year Books

are available for most basic curriculum subjects plus many enrichment areas. For more Good Year Books, contact your local bookseller or educational dealer. For a complete catalog with information about other Good Year Books, please write:

Good Year Books
An imprint of Pearson Learning
299 Jefferson Road, P.O. Box 480
Parsippany, NJ 07054-0480
www.pearsonlearning.com
1-800-321-3106

Cover Illustration: Terry Taylor
Book Design: Elaine Lopez
Interior Illustrations: Jenny Campbell
Design Manager: M. Jane Heelan
Editorial Manager: Suzanne Beason
Executive Editor: Judith Adams

ISBN 0-673-58903-X

2 3 4 5 6 7 8 9 - ML - 07 06 05 04 03 02 01

This Book Is Printed
On Recycled Paper

Preface

As Title I resource teachers with forty-seven years of combined experience, we want to share with you our major reason for writing this book: children. To help a child succeed is one of the most rewarding experiences in life.

We work with many children who, for a variety of reasons, struggle with learning to read. They may enter school as eager learners, but they quickly lose this eagerness. We know from experience as well as from research that children who are not reading by third grade are often destined for failure.

Many of these children, coming from disadvantaged environments, start school with gaps in their learning. Despite the best efforts of their teachers, they continue to struggle. We cannot change what occurred before children entered school, but we can try to close the gaps by explicitly teaching those children a set of basic reading skills, presented in a developmental, sequential format.

Our book assists teachers in this overwhelming job. It provides a road map of crucial reading skills all children should master and gives the teacher a repertoire of techniques specifically intended for use with children who always seem to be lagging behind. Our aim has been to create a resource to help all educators meet the needs of struggling learners in their classrooms.

Our experience with the struggling learner is wide-ranging. While working in our own classrooms, our Title I positions have also taken us into other teachers' classrooms where we have informally observed a variety of instructional approaches. These experiences have been invaluable.

Our interactions with dedicated classroom teachers, as well as their supervisors, principals, and assistant principals, have exposed us to innovative ideas, research, and constructive criticism, all of which have improved our teaching techniques. At conventions, conferences, and workshops, we have heard some of the best and brightest professionals in our field. These people have not only given us ideas, but also validated what we do every day.

So many people have influenced our instructional methods that it would be impossible to name and give credit to every individual. Nonetheless, we would like to acknowledge the many dedicated people whose ideas we have adopted and adapted through the years. We are grateful to be part of this network of educators, a dynamic force that urges us to continue striving to meet the educational needs of all children.

Introduction

Reading is a skill, not a subject, and is the means by which children learn virtually all other subjects.

In the United States, hardly a day goes by without a report about the failures of our education system. The literacy problem is by far the most distressing of all. Teachers are finding it more and more difficult to meet the needs of all their students, and almost every classroom in the country has some struggling learners.

Children enter school eager to learn, yet many are soon thwarted by difficulties with reading. When children do not progress in reading, their self-esteem and confidence suffer. They have trouble not only in reading class, but in every other class that involves a textbook. These children are often carried along in the system, discouraged and falling further behind each year, until they are old enough to drop out of school.

Meeting the Needs of Struggling Learners As Title I resource teachers, we see ourselves as advocates for children. For our work with struggling learners, we have collected and developed a set of teaching techniques that target their special needs.

In our view, learning to read is a developmental, step-by-step process. Mastery of reading skills is not measured by the number of hours children spend in reading instruction, but by the children's success at transferring the step-by-step skills to their long-term memories. This is where struggling learners stumble. They have gaps in their reading skills—specific steps of the process that they have not mastered. When children fail to pick up a particular reading skill, they experience difficulty with reading until someone helps them fix the problem.

Our book is a tool that educators can use to retrace and reteach steps that children may have missed when learning to read. The activities are not meant to take the place of a total reading program; instead, they are a supplemental resource for teachers looking for extra help with their struggling learners. We offer help with four types of reading skills, each dependent on the others and at times overlapping: phonics, vocabulary building, structural analysis, and comprehension.

PHONICS

In recent years, many educators have become aware that phonemic awareness, or the ability to hear the distinct sounds in a spoken word, is a strong predictor for learning to read fluently and successfully. Closely related to phonemic awareness is instruction in phonics—the relationship between patterns of letters in print and those spoken sounds. The phonics instruction we use in the primary grades is systematic, explicit, and code-oriented.

- Systematic phonics instruction builds from concrete principles (one letter/one sound) to more abstract elements.

- Explicit phonics instruction teaches particular rules about letter-sound relationships.

- Code-oriented phonics instruction helps children break the reading "code."

For every phonics skill, from the earliest work with single consonant sounds to later work with irregular vowel spellings and silent consonants, we group and teach similar concepts together, making it easier for children to see the big picture of reading.

Oral Techniques From experience, we know that direct instruction in the sounds of consonants, consonant blends and digraphs, and vowels is best done through oral activities, rather than with the familiar picture-clue worksheets many teachers associate with the term *phonics*.

Mnemonic Aids While directing these oral activities, we suggest mnemonic aids to assist the children in recalling the different sound-letter connections—tricks and reminders that involve the visual, auditory, and kinesthetic modalities (seeing, hearing, and doing) and keep the learning concrete rather than abstract.

VOCABULARY BUILDING

Despite the importance of phonics skills, children who focus exclusively on decoding printed words will not become balanced readers. They also need to construct meaning from what they read. To this end, we must help children build their vocabularies.

Sight Vocabulary Vocabulary building is an ongoing process. In the early stages, our primary goal is to increase sight vocabulary—common words that appear repeatedly in text, which children need to know instantly for fluent reading. These words are already a basic part of children's speaking vocabulary, and they must become part of their early reading vocabulary, too.

Word Meaning As the children's reading ability grows, our goal for vocabulary building shifts. Now we want to help readers develop a reserve of words that will aid in increased comprehension, including

- homophones

- antonyms

- synonyms

- words with multiple meanings

"Active thinking" is the key to effective vocabulary building. Our techniques include encouraging children to use context clues and to visualize or draw pictures showing word meaning. All are ways to actively involve the reader in getting meaning from the page.

STRUCTURAL ANALYSIS

As children develop their reading abilities, their skills need to include structural analysis of words, or the study of word parts. When children can recognize large words as smaller word parts hooked together, they are able to read at a more difficult level. Instead of skipping or guessing at each unfamiliar word, they know they have the tools to pronounce the word correctly. Looking at word parts—whether in compound words or in words with prefixes or suffixes—frequently offers clues to the word's meaning as well.

Building on Root Words Teaching structural analysis starts with word-building activities, such as forming new words by adding parts to root words. Once children become comfortable with the building process, the technique can be reversed; now they can break words into parts and look for clues that indicate meaning.

COMPREHENSION

The ultimate goal of all reading instruction is comprehension: understanding what is being read. It is an ongoing process that begins as soon as children are able to read their first words.

Active Thinking for Comprehension Many struggling learners are so removed from actively thinking about what they read that they become passive word-callers, waiting for the meaning to smack them in the face. When they don't comprehend what they are reading, they have a tendency to continue anyway, satisfied that reading has occurred, even though they gained little or no meaning from the printed page.

Children who understand what they read, on the other hand, use the words to create pictures in their minds. Our oral questioning techniques, visualization methods, use of word clues, and ways to "read between the lines" all help children to actively think about what they read. The outcome is improved comprehension.

How to Use This Book

We have used the techniques in this book primarily with struggling learners in grades 1 to 3. Our techniques support fifteen phonics skills, four vocabulary building skills, six structural analysis skills, and nine comprehension skills.

Finding the Skills We have grouped the first twenty-five skills into three chapters, corresponding to reading levels. The comprehension skills are grouped together in a fourth chapter because the same set of skills overlaps first and second grade.

- Chapter 1. Early Reading: Letter Recognition and Phonemic Awareness

- Chapter 2. First Grade: Word Recognition

- Chapter 3. Second Grade: Toward Reading Fluency

- Chapter 4. Comprehension: Active Thinking About the Text

Step-by-Step Progression The phonics skills and the first vocabulary building skills are presented in a sequential order, showing a developmental, step-by-step progression. However, we do not expect most users to start at the beginning and work their way through every skill with every child. Instead, when teachers see a child having difficulty with a particular reading skill, they can locate that skill in the book and review our techniques for teaching or reteaching it.

Reviewing Problem Areas Struggling learners of all ages can benefit from the reteaching of skills that they may have been exposed to at earlier levels. Thus, you may have a second grader who could benefit from work with an "early reading" skill, or a third grader who needs additional practice with both "first grade" phonics and "second grade" structural analysis skills. The work you do should always be defined by a child's particular needs. If children continue to have difficulty, it may be because they have not mastered one or more of the preceding skills. Our sequential presentation helps you identify these problem areas, so you can back up to close any and all gaps in learning.

Stories for Comprehension The later skills in the sequence—second grade vocabulary and structural analysis, and comprehension skills for both first and second grade—are not strictly ordered, and should be used as children's needs dictate. Some comprehension skills may be taught initially with children at the first-grade reading level, and then retaught and refined as the children progress to more advanced levels. In controlling the vocabulary for the sample comprehension stories, we assume that children are already familiar with the phonics skills for the corresponding reading level.

Daily R-T-P

Struggling learners can be easily overwhelmed. For them, the pace of instruction can seem fast and furious. These children need ample practice and review if they are to transfer each new skill to their long-term memories.

Spaced Practice We find that spaced practice—that is, practice revisited for a brief time daily over several days or even months—is more valuable for struggling learners than continuous, intensive practice over one or two days. To truly learn what is being taught, bright children may require up to five practice sessions; average children may require as many as forty sessions; and most significantly, struggling learners may require as many as eighty.

Quick Daily Review For this reason, we recommend a quick daily review to reinforce any skill you have presented. We use the letters R-T-P as a reminder of review, teach or reteach, and practice—the three steps that give children the chance they need to close gaps in their learning. R-T-P helps them remember what has been taught and sets the stage for what is going to be taught. You decide on the focus of each R-T-P lesson, based on your observations of the children as they are reading aloud. We include the phrase *Daily R-T-P* periodically in these pages as a reminder to consistently use this supportive technique for teaching struggling learners.

Materials for Teaching the Skills

Along with our techniques, we provide many examples of visual aids and teaching tools that are effective for all struggling learners, especially those who are easily distracted: ADD, ADHD, and learning-disabled students. All are materials that we make ourselves, laminating them for repeated use with different students.

Sentence Strips Many techniques call for sentence strips—3-by-24-inch strips with writing guidelines, printed on manila tagboard, available from school supply stores and dealers. We have prepared hundreds of these for our own use, writing the sentences with large, bold print and then laminating the strips.

Using laminated strips, children can make their own marks with water-based markers or highlighters, boxing letters and highlighting words to help them focus on key areas. These marks are then easily wiped away for the next user. Sentence strips present a more hands-on approach to reading for the kinesthetic learner, and also help those who struggle with reading and tracking the smaller print of books and worksheets.

For storage, we have discovered that sentence strips fit perfectly, placed sideways, into the check storage boxes that can be purchased at office supply stores. We group sentences by skill area, with separate boxes for phonics, vocabulary development, structural analysis, and high-frequency sight words. We make dividers with stick-on tabs to further group the sentences, by specific skill, within a box.

Word Cards and Word Lists We have also prepared many word cards and word lists, again using large, bold print on simple index cards or tagboard sheets, and laminating them for repeated use.

Sentence Lists For learners who are reading at the second-grade level, we sometimes type lists of fill-in-the-blank sentences and laminate them. Since students write their answers with water-based markers, we can later erase their work and reuse the same lists.

Story Sheets For work with comprehension skills at both the first- and second-grade levels, we present story sheets—short stories typed or printed on tagboard and laminated for repeated classroom use. The sample stories in chapter 4 can be set up this way. The techniques they demonstrate can also be used with any available reading materials.

Game Boards and Cards Other special teaching tools, including various types of cards and boards illustrated in these pages, are important to the success of our techniques. All can be prepared with readily available school supplies: tagboard or poster board, index cards, colored card stock, and permanent markers.

In Summary

There is an analogy in our profession that reading is like learning how to ride a bike. First, you use training wheels. Next, someone holds the bike to help you balance. With practice, you are able to ride on your own. Our purpose in writing this book is to help teachers provide the "training wheels" and the "balance" for learning to read. With sufficient practice, your students will eventually be able to ride on their own—on their way down the road to a lifetime of learning!

Early Reading

To get ready to read, children should be comfortable with print.

We don't expect babies to walk before they can crawl, yet when children enter school, they are often asked to do things they cannot yet do. Children must be comfortable with print, and with the shapes of the letters of the alphabet, before they can begin to read.

Some children will have had little or no exposure to the printed word at home. If they have not been read to, they won't know the standard conventions of reading a book. Their limited experience with print calls for some catching up. Struggling learners of any age may have gaps that occurred at the kindergarten level. Our techniques help struggling readers become comfortable with print in the following ways:

- **Readiness Skill: Directionality** We train children's eyes to track print correctly, moving from left to right and top to bottom—something they don't automatically know how to do. This is very difficult for some children, and we provide aids to help them correctly follow a line of print.

- **Phonics Skill 1: Upper- and Lowercase Letter Names** Children must be able to visually recognize and know the name of each letter of the alphabet, in both upper- and lowercase forms. To simplify this overwhelming task, we group letters by their visual similarities, and children learn one group before proceeding to the next.

- **Phonics Skill 2: Consonant Sounds** Learning the sounds that consonants stand for is the next step. We teach children that with some consonants, the letter name is a clue to its sound; with the other consonants, mnemonic aids can help children recall the sounds.

- **Phonics Skill 3:** **Beginning and Ending Consonant Sounds** Through an oral technique that raises phonemic awareness, we help children connect the consonant sounds they learned in isolation to the sounds they hear at the beginning and ending of simple words.

- **Phonics Skill 4: Rhyming Words** Children extend their auditory awareness of sounds in words by listening for words that rhyme, or end with the same sounds.

As we present these five skills, we help children learn and link them through a short, daily practice (R-T-P), reteaching as necessary until they have mastered the letter names and basic letter sounds and can recognize the consonant sounds when spoken aloud in easy words and in rhyming words.

DIRECTIONALITY

READINESS SKILL: Track print by following left to right across a printed page, and from the top of the page to the bottom.

Teaching left-to-right and top-to-bottom directionality is of utmost importance to early readers. We need to show them the starting point on a page of text and the direction to take to reach the end of each line, as well as how to switch directions and go down to the next line of print. While modeling this, we also call attention to the spaces between words, which tell where one word ends and the next word begins.

Left-to-Right Tracking Aids

Materials   Colored strip of paper, about 9 by 3 inches, for each child. Write the child's name and draw an arrow pointing to the right under the child's name. Prepare a similar but larger strip for use with a big book.

Tanisha →

Give each child a colored strip to place above or below the printed line being read. For children who have a tendency to reread the same line, placing the colored strip above the line eliminates this problem. Other children find it more comfortable to place the colored strip of paper below the line. Help children choose the appropriate placement.

Point out that the arrow is a reminder of which way they will move their eyes when they read. Because most children know the left-to-right directionality of their names, the name on the strip serves as a second reminder.

Use your larger colored strip and a big book set up before the class to model the correct use of the strip. Explain that any time they get confused about direction, children can look at the colored strip, see the arrow and their name, and know which way to move their eyes.

Demonstrate that children can slide their fingers under each word as they read, pausing at every space between words. As their fingers move from one group of letters to the next, the starting and stopping motion reinforces where one word ends and the next word begins.

Many struggling readers, even older ones, have difficulty tracking print in a left-to-right direction. Regardless of their age, children who reread or skip words or entire lines of print should continue to use a tracking aid until they track print effortlessly. Children will not need this assistance forever; by monitoring their progress, you can help them decide when they are ready to give up their tracking aids.

Some children, especially kinesthetic learners, move their bodies in a left-to-right direction as they read. The body movement reminds them which way to move their eyes. Children should be encouraged to use whichever method works best for them.

UPPER- AND LOWERCASE LETTER NAMES

PHONICS SKILL 1: Recognize and name all the written letters of the alphabet, upper- and lowercase.

Before they can read, children must be able to discriminate among the symbols that we call letters. To reduce the amount of confusion for struggling learners, teach the upper- and lowercase letters separately—uppercase letters first, then lowercase, since many look similar to their uppercase counterpart.

Teaching the Uppercase Letters

Materials   Laminated sentence strips, cut to size to display six letter groups (see top of p. 11); water-based markers

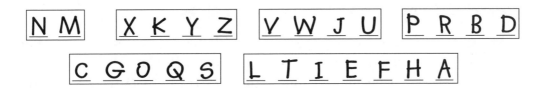

Children who are unfamiliar with print don't see letters, but rather a series of straight and curved lines. To aid children in the discrimination process, we group the uppercase letters by visual similarities. The line under the letters prevents children from reading them upside down.

Present one group at a time. Fold the strip so only the first letter is showing. When children are familiar with the name and shape of the first letter, introduce additional letters in that group by unfolding the paper.

Compare each new letter to the others in that group. How are they the same? different? Introduce a variety of methods for practice of correct letter formation and letter names. For example:

- Using the letter strips, children trace each letter with their fingers and then name it.

- Using the laminated strips, children trace the letters with water-based markers, naming each letter after tracing it.

- Children use their fingers or tools to write letters in the air or in sand, naming each letter they form.

- One child "finger writes" a letter on another child's back. The second child must try to name the letter "written." (This is a more abstract mode of practice and should be used only when children are quite familiar with the letters.)

Teaching the Lowercase Letters

Materials Laminated sentence strips, cut to size to display the six letter groups shown; water-based markers

We also group the lowercase letters by visual similarities. Use the same techniques suggested for teaching the uppercase letters. Once children have mastered naming both sets of letters, they can begin to match the upper- and lowercase forms.

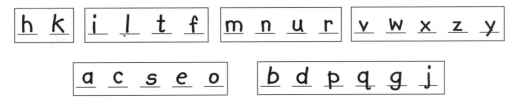

Matching Upper- and Lowercase Letters

Materials Sets of upper- and lowercase letter cards (one set per child), sorted into three groups as shown. Replace the six lowercase letter cards in group 2 (*b, f, h, i, l,* and *t*) with transparent cards cut from acetate sheets. Use a transparency marker to write a letter on each acetate card.

Thirteen of the lowercase letters look exactly or almost exactly like their matching uppercase letters (group 1). Matching these pairs is usually easy for children. Six of the remaining lowercase letters look somewhat similar to the corresponding uppercase letters. We teach these six pairs together (group 2). The seven remaining pairs are the most difficult for struggling learners to match because the letters look nothing alike (group 3).

GROUP 1		GROUP 2	GROUP 3
Look the Same		Somewhat Similar	Look Nothing Alike
C c	U u	B b	A a
J j	V v	F f	D d
K k	W w	H h	E e
M m	X x	I i	G g
O o	Y y	L l	N n
P p	Z z	T t	Q q
S s			R r

- **Teaching the Letters in Group 1** Give children the letter cards from group 1. Have them pull out the thirteen uppercase letters, arrange them in a row, then shuffle the remaining lowercase letter cards and match them to the appropriate uppercase letter. Because the letters in these thirteen pairs are nearly identical in shape, children find they can quickly and easily match letters for an entire half of the alphabet.

- **Teaching the Letters in Group 2** Give children sets of cards from group 2. Children again pull out the six uppercase letter cards and arrange them in a row. They shuffle the remaining six acetate cards, then match them by placing an acetate card on top of the corresponding uppercase card.

The transparent card allows children to see that the lowercase letter fits almost on top of its matching uppercase letter, as if it is "part" of that letter. Matching group 2 cards is somewhat more abstract and difficult than matching group 1 cards.

• **Teaching the Letters in Group 3** When children have mastered groups 1 and 2, they can match nineteen out of twenty-six pairs of letters. Only seven difficult pairs remain, so the task is now much less overwhelming for the struggling learner. Tell children that these pairs of letters do not look anything alike, and we just have to "look at and know" them.

Introduce only one pair at a time. After practicing each new "look-at-and-know" pair, children insert them into their collection of cards from groups 1 and 2. They continue until they have mastered all of group 3. Children now have a complete set of letter cards they can use to practice matching.

• DAILY R-T-P •

Children shuffle complete sets of upper- and lowercase letter cards and match all the lowercase letters to the uppercase letters, orally naming each letter as they make a pair. This offers practice with visual recognition of all letters as well as a review of their names.

CONSONANT SOUNDS

PHONICS SKILL 2: Say the sounds represented by the consonant letters.

To be able to read, children need to be able to say consonant letter sounds in isolation and eventually as part of a word. Struggling learners are sometimes confused by the idea that letters have both a name *and* a sound.

At this point children should already know the name of each letter. Fortunately, fourteen of the consonants have sounds that are closely related to their names. When we say the letter's name, we also hear its sound, either at the beginning or end of the name.

For example, when we say the name of the letter *b,* we also pronounce the /b/ sound at the beginning of the name. Because children make this link fairly easily, we start by teaching the letter sounds of these "easy fourteen" consonants. Once children have mastered the "easy fourteen," they are ready to tackle the other seven consonants whose sounds are more difficult because we don't hear them in the letter's name.

Note that we include the letter *r* with the second group. Although we do technically hear /r/ at the end of the letter's name, our mouth is in a different position than we use for /r/ as a beginning sound, and children do not readily link the sound with the letter's name.

CONSONANT LETTER SOUNDS

Hear the Sound in the Letter's Name

b d f j k l m n p s t v x z

Don't Hear the Sound in the Letter's Name

c g h qu r w y

Teaching the sounds of consonants should always be an oral activity, with children saying and listening for the names of consonant letters. Paper-and-pencil activities make it much harder for struggling learners to connect the letter names to the letter sounds.

Teaching Sounds We Hear in Letter Names

Materials   Lowercase letter cards for the consonants *b, d, f, j, k, l, m, n, p, s, t, v, x,* and *z*

Tell the children to listen closely as they say the names of these letters, and they will hear the letter's sound.

Hold up one letter card, for example the *d*. Children look at the card, say the letter name, and think about the sound of *d*. Have the children chant, "This is what the *d* says: /d/, /d/, /d/." Note that the teacher doesn't name the consonant letter or say the sound; only the children do.

Teach children to finish saying each consonant sound with their mouths open. This way, when they begin reading, they will be ready for the rest of the word. This mouth position will be natural for some letters, but harder to remember for a letter such as *m*.

Teaching Sounds We Don't Hear in Letter Names

Materials   Lowercase letter cards for the consonants *c, g, h, q, r, w,* and *y*. Modify the *q* card by writing the letter *u* after it.

Teach children the following mnemonic aids to help them recall the sounds of these seven letters. You may want to teach only one or two letters at a time.

As children learn each letter sound, remind them to finish saying the sound with their mouths open so when they are reading, they will be ready for the rest of a word.

For the letters *c* and *g*, we teach the more common hard sounds /k/ as in *cat* and /g/ as in *go*. The soft sounds /s/ for *c* and /j/ for *g* are presented as a first-grade skill.

Mnemonic Aids

- The sound of *c* is different from its name. Children could think of the letters *c* and *k* as "twin sisters." They don't look alike, but they both have the same sound, /k/.

- Because of their similar letter names, the sounds of *g* and *j* are often confused. Children can learn the chant "G-O says go" to remind them of the sound of *g* as in *go*.

- The sound of *h* is different from its name. The chant "H-O-T says hot" reminds children that *h* has the sound /h/ as in *hot*.

- To explain the letter pair *qu*, you might say that the letter *q* is almost always found with a *u*; they are linked the way a *queen* is linked to a king. Thinking of the word *queen* reminds children that *qu* has the sound /kw/ as in *queen*.

- The sound of *r* can be problematic because some children have trouble articulating it. It is especially hard to hear clearly at the end of words, such as *for* and *car*. Focus instead on the /r/ sound at the beginning of words, and teach children to think of the word *run*. That is, *r* has the sound /r/ as in *run*.

- The sound of *w* is completely different from its name. A gimmick to help children remember this sound is to point to a window, preferably one that opens by raising and lowering it. Run your finger up and down the lines of the letter *w*, pointing out that *w* goes up and down like a window. Children can then remember that the letter *w* has the sound /w/ as in *window*.

- The sound of *y* is different from its name, too. Teaching children to connect *y* with the word *yes* reminds them that *y* has the sound /y/ as in *yes*.

◆ DAILY R-T-P ◆

Every day, have children review the consonants they have learned thus far. As they master each new sound, add it to the daily oral practice until children are reviewing all twenty-one consonant letter sounds.

BEGINNING AND ENDING CONSONANT SOUNDS

PHONICS SKILL 3: Say and identify beginning and ending consonant letter sounds in simple words.

Through techniques that focus on phonemic awareness, children now extend what they know about the names and sounds of consonant letters as they listen for the consonant sounds in simple words. These activities should always be oral, with children repeating simple words after you and listening for the beginning or ending sounds.

Start by focusing on beginning sounds, which tend to be easier for children to hear; later you can extend the skill to ending sounds. To ease the task for struggling learners, first present only words with beginning sounds that are linked to the name of the letter. Later you can introduce words that start with the more difficult consonants.

As needed, continue to review consonant sounds in isolation, helping children connect the sounds with the letter names or with the mnemonic aids they have learned (Phonics Skill 2).

Teaching Beginning Sounds Linked to Letter Names

Materials   Resource list of one-syllable words that start with one of the "easy fourteen" consonants, with a sound linked to the letter's name

For this activity, you might seat children where they can see a display of consonants for reference.

SIMPLE WORDS WITH BEGINNING SOUNDS LINKED TO LETTER NAMES

bag	dip	jet	met	pet	tag
bat	dot	job	mom	pig	tap
bed	dug	kid	mug	pin	ten
big	fan	kit	nap	pop	tip
box	fat	lap	net	pup	top
bug	fed	let	not	sad	tub
bun	fit	lip	nut	sat	tug
dad	fox	lot	pan	sit	van
did	fun	map	pat	sob	vet
dig	jam	men	pen	sun	zip

- Say a simple word from the list, such as *map*.

- Children repeat the word and think about the sound they hear at the beginning. They may have to repeat the word more than once.

- Children then say the initial consonant sound /m/ in isolation, and link that sound to the name of the letter *m*. Reinforce this connection by helping them notice that their mouths are in the same position when they name the letter *m* and say the /m/ sound.

- Continue with other simple words from this list.

After repeated practice, reverse the process. You say a consonant sound, such as /f/, and the children repeat it two or three times. Children then suggest a word that begins with the /f/ sound, such as *fun,* and tell you what letter the word *fun* begins with. Again, help them match the sound to the letter name by recognizing that their mouths are in the same position when they say each one: the name *f* and the sound /f/.

Teaching Beginning Sounds Not Linked to Letter Names

Materials   Resource list of one-syllable words that start with a consonant whose sound we *don't* hear in the letter's name

As you orally present words from this list, remember that struggling learners may have difficulty connecting these beginning sounds with the corresponding letters because they don't hear the sounds in the letter names. Remind children to use the mnemonic aids they have learned to help them recall the sounds of the letters *c, g, h, qu, r, w,* and *y.*

- Say a simple word from the list, such as *hat.*

- Children repeat the word, more than once as needed, and think about the sound they hear at the beginning.

SIMPLE WORDS WITH BEGINNING SOUNDS NOT LINKED TO LETTER NAMES

can	gas	hat	hop	rat	web
cap	get	hem	hot	red	wet
cat	got	hen	hug	rib	wig
cot	gull	hid	quick	rug	win
cub	gum	him	quit	run	yam
cup	had	hip	quiz	wag	yes
cut	ham	hit	rag	wax	yet

- When they say the sound /h/ in isolation, they should be able to match that sound to the letter *h* by using the mnemonic aid "H-O-T says hot," and say that *hat* begins with an *h*.

After repeated practice of words with these letters, reverse the process. You say a consonant sound, such as /w/, and the children repeat it several times. Children then suggest a word that begins with the /w/ sound, such as *wig,* and name the letter the word begins with. Using the mnemonic aid they have learned, they should say the word *wig* begins with the letter *w* because they remember that *w* goes up and down like a window.

Teaching Ending Sounds

| Materials | Resource list of one-syllable words with the focus on ending sounds |

Struggling learners often have trouble with ending sounds in words because they don't say them—they leave them off. Teach them to say the ending sounds in words clearly, cupping a hand over your ear any time they drop the ending sound. This simple motion tells children to repeat the word, clearly pronouncing the sound at the end.

SIMPLE WORDS WITH FOCUS ON ENDING SOUNDS

cub	if	bell	can	gas	box
rib	off	hill	fun	us	fix
sob	puff	pal	ten	yes	tax
bed	big	hum	cup	cat	buzz
hid	jog	ram	map	fit	fizz
mad	rug	sum	top	nut	quiz

Once children have mastered beginning sounds, they should encounter few other problems when extending the skill to ending sounds since they are using what they already know about letter-sound relationships. Perhaps the best way to focus on ending sounds is to listen for rhyming words (Phonics Skill 4).

RHYMING WORDS

PHONICS SKILL 4: Identify spoken words that rhyme.

On this level, rhyming is a phonemic awareness skill and is entirely auditory. That is, children are not *reading* words; instead they are *hearing* spoken words and identifying those that end the same way. While they listen for ending consonant sounds, they are also starting to hear the middle vowel sounds that are part of the rhyme. Limiting these to short vowel sounds gives children practice with the type of words they will encounter when they begin reading.

Listening for Rhyming Words

Materials   Resource list of simple rhyming words

Say a group of simple rhyming words. Children then repeat the words to hear the singsong sounds.

To make this a kinesthetic technique, teach children to use hand motions to see if two word endings match:

- Have them put out their hands as if to make a balance scale while they say two words. For example, children say *top* as they put out one hand, then say *pop* as they put out the other hand.

- As they look at their extended hands, children will hear that *top* and *pop* have the same ending sounds.

Connecting the sounds with physical motions is especially helpful for struggling learners because it gets them actively involved in what they are learning.

When children are able to identify a variety of rhyming words, start to include in each group one word that doesn't rhyme with the others. Children must tell you which word does not rhyme. This helps them learn to discriminate between ending sounds.

RHYMING WORDS

can	bad	ham	bet	cot	bug
fan	dad	jam	jet	dot	dug
man	had	ram	met	got	hug
ran	mad	Pam	set	hot	mug
van	sad	Sam	wet	pot	rug
bat	cap	den	big	cop	cub
mat	lap	hen	dig	hop	hub
pat	map	men	pig	mop	rub
rat	nap	pen	rig	pop	sub
sat	tap	ten	wig	top	tub

First Grade

Beginning reading is like soaking up water with a sponge—keep the code simple and children will absorb it all.

When children are struggling at a first-grade reading level, you can help them by giving systematic instruction and practice in explicit phonics skills. Children who are still having trouble with consonant sounds will benefit from the work we suggest in chapter 1, Early Reading. However, the most troublesome phonics skills at the first-grade level usually involve the vowel sounds.

Unlike the consonants, which are remarkably consistent in standing for a single sound, vowels can stand for different sounds in different words. We teach children to follow two simple steps when facing a new word: (1) count the vowels, and (2) notice the pattern of the vowels.

We start with three phonics skills that each present a general vowel pattern children should learn to recognize.

- **Phonics Skill 5: Short Vowels** One vowel alone in the middle of a word usually indicates a short-vowel sound (*cap, bed, tip, hot, rub*).

- **Phonics Skill 6: Long Vowels: Two Vowels Together** Two vowels together usually indicate that the first vowel has a long sound and the second is silent (*rain, boat, toe, feet, meal, pie*).

- **Phonics Skill 7: Long Vowels: Silent *e*** One vowel with a silent *e* at the end of the word (we call this the "jump-over" pattern) usually indicates a long-vowel sound (*same, here, mine, vote, tune*).

In addition to these vowel sounds, we present three other skills crucial to readers at a first-grade level.

- **Phonics Skill 8: Consonant Blends and Digraphs** Once they are thoroughly familiar with single-consonant sounds, children begin to recognize groups of two or three consonants—the digraphs and blends—that stand for a single or blended sound.

- **Vocabulary Skill 1: High-Frequency Words** Beginning readers are often expected to learn by sight a list of 220 high-frequency words. We simplify the process by classifying that list into two categories: decodable words and "look-at-and-know" words.

   With the decodable words, children simply apply their previously learned vowel skills. The look-at-and-know words don't follow the rules that first graders have learned for short- and long-vowel sounds, but we help young readers discriminate among them by grouping sets of words with similar spellings or similar sounds.

- **Phonics Skill 9: Hard and Soft *c* and *g*** When children first learned to connect consonants with spoken sounds, they learned the hard sounds for the letters *c* and *g*. Now we teach the soft sounds, showing children that the following vowel usually indicates which sound to use. In this way children see that while there are exceptions to phonics rules, these exceptions often have their own patterns.

Children will master these six skills only over time. Giving them quick daily reviews, using the R-T-P format (review, teach or reteach, practice), improves the percentage of mastery learning. Remember that consistent review is especially important to fill in the gaps for struggling learners.

One way to incorporate a quick review into daily instruction is to set up a wall chart headed Which One Is It? With this chart, children categorize the words they are studying into one of four groups: look-at-and-know (represented by a pair of eyes), one vowel (short-vowel sound), two vowels together (long-vowel sound), and jump-over pattern (long vowel and silent *e*).

Set up the chart on oversize paper or poster board and laminate it. Then, use a water-based marker to write words in the columns so you can later rub them off for a fresh start. You may also reproduce small copies of the chart on index cards for children to keep at their desks or at home, to use as reminders of the vowel patterns when they encounter a word they don't know.

Display this chart prominently in the room. As you introduce and practice each skill, refer to the appropriate section on the chart. Whenever children can't identify the proper category for a particular word, this is your cue to reteach the relevant skills.

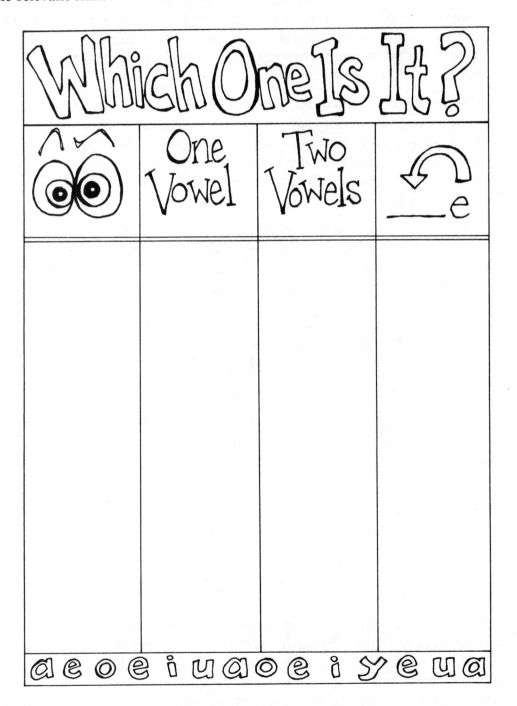

SHORT VOWELS

PHONICS SKILL 5: Read words with one vowel, signaling a short-vowel sound.

Many children have difficulty learning the short-vowel sounds, which are hard to hear because they sound very similar. If children don't hear the short-vowel sounds correctly, they cannot remember and duplicate them.

These five vowel sounds (short *a*, *e*, *i*, *o*, and *u*) are often taught as five separate skills; we prefer to teach all five together. Note that children don't need to know the terms *short vowel* and *long vowel*, but only the different sounds suggested by the different vowel patterns.

Teaching the Short-Vowel Sounds

Materials   Teaching card listing the five vowels and the corresponding trigger words, as illustrated

$$a \rightarrow at$$
$$e \rightarrow edge$$
$$i \rightarrow in$$
$$o \rightarrow on$$
$$u \rightarrow up$$

To teach the short-vowel sounds, use trigger words with accompanying hand motions. This technique is especially helpful for children who have problems with auditory discrimination, as the hand motions trigger the auditory memory of the correct vowel sound.

Short Vowel	Trigger Word	Hand Motion
/a/	at (the desk)	Both palms up on desktop
/e/	edge (of the desk)	One palm touches edge of desk
/i/	in (the desk)	Hand moves inward over desktop
/o/	on (the desk)	One hand, fingertips down, on desk
/u/	up (above the desk)	One hand, fingertips raised, moving toward ceiling

Introduce these hand motions to children who are seated at a desk. Point to the *a* card and say, "Short *a* says /a/." Then point to the trigger word, saying the phrase and making the corresponding motion. Repeat for each vowel. In subsequent work with short-vowel words, the hand motion triggers the phrase for the children, and they are able to say the corresponding short-vowel sound.

Reading Short-Vowel Words

Materials   Laminated cards for short-vowel words (prepare from list, p. 25). When making word cards, always use large, bold print to help children discriminate the letters.

Once children are comfortable with the hand motions, present short-vowel word cards, mixing them randomly. To read these words, children say the first consonant sound, then use the hand motion as they say the vowel sound, and finally say the ending consonant sound. For example:

sat

- Children say /s/ for the letter *s*.
- They see the *a*, remember the phrase *at the desk,* do the hand motion, and say /a/ as in *at*.
- They say /t/ for the letter *t*.
- They repeat the three letter sounds, sliding them together to form the word *sat*.

Struggling learners often need lots of practice with sliding the sounds together, but this letter-by-letter approach helps them lock in the correct spelling of short-vowel words. After children have the five short-vowel sounds stored in their long-term memories, most will stop using the hand motions.

• DAILY R-T-P •

Introduce the Which One Is It? chart (p. 22). Explain that the words children will be reading belong in one of the columns on the chart. Pass out word cards and ask children to count the vowels in each word. Write some of the words in the *One Vowel* column.

Children begin to recognize that when they see one vowel in a word, they will usually say the short sound, regardless of which vowel it is. Those who fail to master this critical skill will continue to experience difficulty in reading.

WORDS WITH SHORT-VOWEL SOUNDS

/a/	/e/	/i/	/o/	/u/
bat	bed	big	hop	bug
cat	fed	dig	pop	dug
fat	red	pig	top	hug
hat	Ted	wig	cot	rug
mat	den	fin	dot	tug
sat	hen	pin	got	but
bad	Jen	win	hot	cut
dad	Ken	bit	lot	nut
had	men	fit	not	cub
mad	pen	hit	pot	tub
sad	ten	sit	mom	fun
bag	get	quit	Tom	bun
rag	jet	lip	box	run
ham	let	rip	fox	sun
jam	met	tip	job	cup
Sam	net	did	Bob	pup
can	pet	kid		
Jan	set	rid		
man	vet	him		
ran	wet	Kim		
van	yes	Tim		
cap	web	bib		
lap		rib		
map				
nap				

LONG VOWELS: TWO VOWELS TOGETHER

PHONICS SKILL 6: Read words with two vowels together, signaling a long-vowel sound.

Children often learn a rhyme to help them remember this long-vowel phonics principle: "Two vowels go walking, the first one does the talking." However, many children don't understand what that really means. We teach the skill according to our two-step plan: (1) count the vowels, and (2) notice the pattern of the vowels. We also teach a hand motion that helps kinesthetic learners focus on the pattern.

Teaching the Pattern of Two Vowels Together

Materials   Resource list of long-vowel words with two vowels together (p. 27)

On the board, write a long-vowel word with the pattern "two vowels together." Ask a volunteer to count the vowels. Then teach children to hold up the index and middle fingers on one hand, symbolizing that the word has two vowels next to each other.

Explain that in this pattern, the first vowel usually says its name, and the second one is silent. The simple motion of holding up two fingers together helps children focus on the two-vowel pattern in the word. Counting the vowels helps children track in the correct direction, so they correctly identify the first vowel that will "say its name," and the second vowel that is silent.

When children are looking at words with two vowels together, ask them, "What vowels are jumping out at you?" This helps them to zero in on the double-vowel pattern.

This is a good time to introduce the technique of boxing letters in a word. Boxing two vowels together reminds struggling readers that the letters must stay together and that together they make one sound. To further reinforce the pattern, tell children to put a slash through the second vowel to remind them that it is silent.

For example, write the word *soap* on the board.

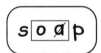

Ask the children to count the vowels, and lead them in holding up two fingers to indicate the pattern. Call on a volunteer to draw a box around the two vowels and to mark out the one that is silent. Now children can read the word because they know that the letters *oa* have the sound of long *o*.

Repeat with other two-vowel words until children seem comfortable with the pattern. Remind children that the letter *y* is sometimes a vowel, as in *-ay* words.

Reading Long-Vowel Words

Materials   Laminated cards for long-vowel words with two vowels together (prepare from list below); water-based markers

Distribute laminated word cards and markers to the children. Encourage them to count the vowels *and* use the finger motions to indicate the pattern. Children might also draw boxes around the two vowels as they practice reading the words, a technique they enjoy that also keeps them actively involved. Knowing how and where to draw the boxes helps them connect sounds to spelling.

To help visual learners who are struggling with these long-vowel patterns, try writing the letters *ai, ay, ee, ea, ie, oa, oe,* and *ue* on the index and middle fingers of a latex glove. This gives them the actual patterns on their fingers rather than having to recall them.

To help ADD and ADHD students focus on print, provide a penlight that they can shine on the two vowels together.

LONG-VOWEL WORDS WITH TWO VOWELS TOGETHER

rain	bay	bee	pea	die
paid	day	Lee	sea	lie
bait	hay	see	deal	pie
wait	Jay	feet	heal	tie
hail	Kay	meet	meal	died
mail	may	heel	seal	dies
pail	pay	peel	beak	pies
sail	say	teen	leak	tied
tail	way		weak	ties
			bead	
boat	doe	due	lead	
coat	hoe	Sue	read	
soap	Joe		mean	
foam	toe		team	
moan	toes		leap	
			meat	

Work in sight of the Which One Is It? chart, with a pool of short-vowel and long-vowel word cards on the table. Children take turns choosing a card from the pool to read.

Explain that each word belongs in one of the columns of the chart. As children read each word and identify its pattern, write it in the correct column. At this point, you will have words only in the *One Vowel* and *Two Vowels* columns.

LONG VOWELS: SILENT E

PHONICS SKILL 7: Read words with one vowel and a silent *e* at the end, signaling a long-vowel sound.

A phrase commonly used to describe this sound/spelling pattern is "sneaky, silent *e*." While the phrase may be appealing, many children don't understand how to apply it when they are reading words. You can teach this long-vowel principle to struggling learners with another hand motion that helps them recognize the pattern.

Teaching the Jump-Over Pattern

Materials — Resource list of long-vowel words with the jump-over pattern (p. 29); small self-stick labels (optional)

Before you start the activity, write an *e* on the tip of your right thumb. Then present on the board a word with the long-vowel, silent *e* pattern, such as *kite*. After children count the vowels in this word, show them your right hand in a closed fist, with the palm of the hand facing them, fingers folded down and thumb up.

Point out that the folded-down fingers act as the first letters in the word, while the thumb represents the silent *e* at the end. With your hand in this formation, wiggle your thumb while explaining that the *e* "jumps over" the consonant to the first vowel in the word to make it say its name. Children, themselves eager jumpers, easily relate to the jump-over pattern.

To further help children who are visual learners, print letters on self-stick labels and stick these on the knuckles of your folded-down fingers, thus showing the letters of the entire word on the fingers.

Continue to present words with the jump-over pattern. Encourage children to make the same hand motion with their own fist to help them focus on the pattern as they read these words together.

Note that a number of common words, such as *have, come, give,* and *love,* are exceptions to the jump-over pattern. Children will learn many of these as sight words when studying the high-frequency word lists of Vocabulary Skill 1 later in this chapter.

LONG-VOWEL WORDS WITH THE JUMP-OVER PATTERN

bake	sale	bike	line	cute
same	tame	time	side	tube
cake	pale	pile	wide	tune
make	wade	nine	hike	rude
lake	save	mile	Mike	rule
cave	take	mine		mule
rake	wave	ride	cone	huge
game	wake	five	rope	use
quake	Kate	kite	bone	Luke
hate	Jake	pipe	poke	
name		ripe	vote	
gate	here	bite	note	
came	Gene	fine	joke	
	Pete	life	home	
		dime	hope	
		hide	cube	

Drawing Boxes and Arrows

Materials Laminated cards for long-vowel words with the jump-over pattern (prepare from list, p. 29); water-based markers

As suggested for the two-vowel pattern (Phonics Skill 6), you can help children focus on print by asking them to box in each letter or combination of letters that stand for a single sound in a word. You can also introduce the arrow as a written symbol of the jump-over pattern. So, for example, write the word *bake* on the board. Ask children to box each letter that makes a sound.

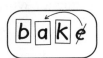

Children draw boxes around the *b*, the *a*, and the *k*; then they put a slash through the silent *e* and draw an arrow above the word, from the *e* back to the *a*. Through this technique, they focus on the relationship between sounds and spelling.

• DAILY R-T-P •

Present a mixture of cards with one-vowel, two-vowel, and "jump-over" words. As children take turns reading the words and identifying the pattern, write each word on the Which One Is It? chart. Teach or reteach skills as needed.

If, during review and practice, children are slow to recognize the jump-over pattern, ask them, "What do you see at the end of that word?" This helps them focus on the silent *e* and remember the pattern.

CONSONANT BLENDS AND DIGRAPHS

PHONICS SKILL 8: Read words with initial and final consonant blends and consonant digraphs.

When two consonants appear together in a word, they are either a *blend* or a *digraph*. Consonant blends are what the name suggests—two consonant sounds blended together. Consonant digraphs, on the other hand, stand for an entirely new sound: /ch/, /th/, /sh/, /wh/.

Blends and digraphs appear at both the beginning and end of words. Initial blends and digraphs, like the single-consonant sounds, can be taught in isolation. However, many final blends, such as *-ft*, *-nt*, *-nk*, *-ng*, and *-mp*, are difficult to pronounce in isolation and are better taught as part of a word.

Teaching Initial Blends and Digraphs

Materials   Blend and digraph strips, made by printing letter combinations in two vertical columns on both sides of cards about 9 by 3 inches. On the strips, group letter combinations to emphasize their visual and auditory similarities: put the *l* blends together, the *r* blends together, and so on.

bl	br
cl	cr
fl	dr
gl	fr
pl	gr
sl	pr
	tr

Front

sc	ch
sk	sh
sm	th
sn	wh
sp	
st	scr
sw	spr
tw	str
	thr

Back

For quick daily oral practice, present the strips and ask children to touch the letters while reading the sounds. Through this practice, children come to see the letters as "locked together" while they hear the blended or new sound. Teach them to complete the sound with their mouths open, so their mouths are ready to say the rest of the word.

Once children become comfortable with reading these initial blends and digraphs, say the sound and ask them to touch or write the correct blend or digraph.

Focusing on Blends and Digraphs

Materials   Laminated cards for words with blends and digraphs (prepare from lists, pp. 32–33); water-based markers or highlighters

Give each child one or more cards and ask which two or three letters together in each word have one sound. Children draw boxes around those letters or use highlighters to accent the blends and digraphs. The boxes and highlighted print make letters stand out for easier reading.

To decode the rest of the word, children continue to follow the two steps of (1) counting the vowels and (2) noticing the vowel pattern. This technique reviews Phonics Skills 5, 6, and 7 for vowel sounds while also keeping struggling readers actively involved and focused on the print.

WORDS WITH INITIAL CONSONANT BLENDS

black	clap	flag	glad	plan	slam
blade	class	flake	glass	plane	sled
blast	clean	flame	Glen	plate	sleep
blaze	click	flat	glide	play	sleeve
bleed	cliff	flea	globe	please	slide
blink	clock	flip		plum	slime
block	club	fluff		plus	slip

brag	crab	drag	frame	grab	press
brain	crack	dream	free	grade	pride
brave	cream	dress	freeze	grass	print
breeze	creek	drink	fries	gray	prize
brick	creep	drip	frog	green	
bride	crib	drive	from	greet	
	crop	drop	froze	grin	

track	scab	skate	smash	snack	speak
trade	scale	skid	smell	snail	speed
trap	scope	skin	smile	snake	spell
treat	Scott	skip	smog	snap	spend
tree	scuff	skunk	smoke	sneak	spill
trick				sneeze	spin
trip				snip	spot

stack	sweep	twig	scrap	sprain	strap
steal	sweet	twin	scrape	spray	street
steam	swell	twist	scream		strike
step	swift		screen		stripe
stick	swim		scrub		
stop	swing				

WORDS WITH FINAL CONSONANT BLENDS

last	raft	belt	ant	kept	bump
past	draft	felt	sent	crept	dump
nest	gift	melt	tent	slept	jump
rest	lift	quilt	went		plump
cost	drift		hint	ask	stump
lost	left		mint	desk	camp
must	soft		hunt		lamp
beast			paint		stamp

WORDS WITH CONSONANT DIGRAPHS

Initial Digraphs

chat	ship	thin	when
chin	shop	that	which
chip	shut	then	whip
chop	sheep	this	white
check	shade	these	wheat
chain	shape	those	wheel
cheek	shake	them	
chase	shine	thank	
chose		thick	
		three	
		throat	
		throne	

Final Digraphs

rich	cash	bath
each	dash	math
peach	crash	path
reach	trash	Beth
teach	dish	with
speech	wish	teeth
	brush	
bench	crush	king
lunch	fresh	ring
		sing
catch		thing
scratch		long
		strong

• DAILY R-T-P •

Provide a stack of word cards with consonant blends and digraphs. Children take turns drawing a card. After they read each word and identify its pattern, they write the word in the correct column of the Which One Is It? chart.

HIGH-FREQUENCY WORDS

VOCABULARY SKILL 1: Read 220 words that appear with high
frequency in standard reading materials.

Research has identified 220 words that constitute a majority of all the
words found in written material for the early grades. Some programs treat these
as sight words, expecting beginning readers to recognize each one visually, with
few oral clues. This expectation sets up many children for failure, especially
struggling learners.

We suggest another approach. First, we divide the list of high-frequency
words into two general categories, decodable words and look-at-and-know or
sight words. Then, within each category, we group together all the words that
follow a particular sound/spelling pattern.

After considerable practice with these groups, we take words from both
categories and focus on "confusable" words—those words that children often
confuse because the spelling is so similar. We help children focus on the
differences between these similar words, reminding them that they can always
find clues in the printed letters.

Teaching Decodable High-Frequency Words

Materials   Laminated lists of decodable high-frequency words (prepare
from lists A–E, p. 35), or laminated word cards

Almost half of the 220 high-frequency words are decodable using first-
grade phonics generalizations; that is, they follow the short- and long-vowel
patterns of Phonics Skills 5, 6, and 7 and may include consonant blends or
digraphs (Phonics Skill 8). These decodable high-frequency words are arranged
in five lists that represent five levels of difficulty, based on the frequency with
which they appear in beginning reading materials.

Distribute word lists to the children. Present List A first; as children master
these words, move on to the next level. As children take turns reading the
words aloud to you, they count the vowels and look for the vowel pattern. Is it
one vowel? two vowels together? or the silent *e* jump-over pattern? For
example:

like   Children count the vowels (two) and notice the silent *e*
jump-over pattern. This pattern tells them that the
i will say its name. They read the word.

| red | Children count the vowels and notice only one *e*. This tells them that the vowel sound is /e/ as in *edge*. They read the word. |

| blue | Children count the vowels (two) and notice two vowels together. This pattern tells them that the *u* will say its name. They read the word. |

If children are having difficulties, suggest that they use the hand motions they learned as reminders of the short- and long-vowel sounds. With enough practice, children will be able to read these words without stopping to decode them; they will know them automatically, just as if they were sight words.

DECODABLE HIGH-FREQUENCY WORDS

List A	List B	List C	List D	List E
at	black	fast	ask	them
am	as	had	that	then
an		has	thank	when
can				went
ran	came	made	take	
and	may	ate	gave	clean
		say		these
	yes			
make	get		well	
play	let	ten	tell	drink
			best	think
help	three	please		bring
red	eat	read	sleep	pick
		green	keep	which
see	did			
here	sit	five	with	those
	if		this	
it	his	wish		use
in	him	sing	white	
is	will	six	write	
big		its		
	stop		off	
ride	from	hot		
like	on	got	just	
		not	much	
up		long	must	
jump				
run		goes		
blue		us		
		but		
		cut		

Teaching Look-at-and-Know Words

Materials   Laminated lists of look-at-and-know high-frequency words (prepare from lists A–E, p. 37)

The remainder of the 220 high-frequency words cannot be sounded out using the first-grade short- and long-vowel rules; counting the vowels and noticing their pattern will not help. Hence, children must simply memorize them as sight words.

Again these words are arranged in five lists, easiest to most difficult. Within each list, we specifically group together words with similar spellings or similar vowel sounds so children can easily see the relationship among them.

For a quick oral drill, start with words from List A. Focus on groups of similar words, encouraging children to use what they know to figure out what they don't know. For example, many children will be able to read the word *to*. Help them build on this knowledge to figure out *too, two, do,* and *you*. As children master the words on List A, continue with Lists B through E.

• DAILY R·T·P •

With children gathered near the Which One Is It? chart, write any high-frequency word on the board. Children count the number of vowels and look for the vowel pattern: one vowel (they hold up one finger); two vowels together (they hold up two fingers); or silent *e* (they hold up a closed fist with the thumb sticking up).

If the word follows one of these patterns, a volunteer writes the word under the appropriate heading and everyone reads the word. If the word doesn't follow these patterns, children know that it is a look-at-and-know word. A volunteer then writes the word in that column of the chart and everyone reads it.

As children write each word, ask the question, "How did you know that? Prove it!" This encourages children to support their answers by stating the phonics pattern they are using.

LOOK-AT-AND-KNOW HIGH-FREQUENCY WORDS

List A	List B	List C	List D	List E
to	or	open	out	where
too	for	over	about	there
two			found	their
do	work	pretty	round	
you	her	funny	around	right
				light
me	put	new	they	
we				both
he	by	your	far	
be	my	four		what
she	fly	our	full	want
	try		pull	
so	buy	who		carry
go		why	kind	
no	laugh		find	seven
		start		eight
come	always	first	one	
some	away		once	does
	today	into		done
good		upon	only	don't
look	was			
	saw	give	before	hurt
all	draw	live	because	
call		have		myself
fall	old		own	
small	cold	of	know	would
	hold		grow	could
are		soon	show	should
	said		yellow	
I		any		wash
a	how	many	were	warm
	now			
the	down	again	been	after
	brown			better
little			walk	never
			talk	every
				very
				under
				together

Distinguishing Confusable Words

Materials Groups of confusable high-frequency words, listed on chart paper or laminated cards (see list below); paper and pencil

Children tend to confuse many of the high-frequency words because the print looks almost the same. Grouping together such confusable words helps children focus on all the individual letters, rather than just quickly looking at the whole configuration and guessing.

For example, children often confuse *want* and *went*. First focus on the word *want;* point to it on the list and have children say it, spell it orally, and write it. Then, add the word *went* and practice both words together. Be sure to have children say the words, spell them orally, and write each one.

Continue to practice pairs and small groups of these words as a short, rapid, daily drill.

CONFUSABLE HIGH-FREQUENCY WORDS

come	think	but	for	over
some	thank	put	four	open
			before	
first	cold	why		of
fast	could	who	wish	off
	would		wash	
he	should	were		no
her		where	all	on
here	has	when	fall	
	was	what	small	one
every	saw			once
very	say	went	those	only
never		want	these	
ever	go			us
	goes	now	there	use
walk		how	their	
wake	do	know		full
talk	does	own	the	pull
take	done		they	
	don't	new	then	at
or		knew		ate
our				
your				

Reading High-Frequency Words in Phrases

Materials   Resource lists of high-frequency words (pp. 35 and 37), to include in phrases written on the board

Many of the high-frequency words are difficult to learn in isolation because they have little or no meaning taken by themselves. It is often easier for children to learn these words when they are presented in phrases and sentences that provide context and meaning.

On the board, write phrases that offer context clues and that have a controlled vocabulary, using only words that are decodable or words from the look-at-and-know list. For example, to attach meaning to the word *all,* write phrases such as *all of us* and *all the dogs.* To attach meaning to the word *for,* write phrases such as *a cake for me* and *run for help.*

To check for understanding, listen as children read the phrases orally. As children actively think about what the words mean and picture the context, they discover that they can get meaning from print. This is the beginning of comprehension.

Reading High-Frequency Words in Sentences

Materials   Laminated sentence strips (see suggested sentences, pp. 40–42); water-based markers or highlighters

For further practice with the high-frequency words, provide sentences on laminated strips, again using a controlled vocabulary with decodable and look-at-and-know high-frequency words. In some sentences, include pairs of confusable words.

As children take turns reading the sentences orally, they can box in (or highlight) letters that make one sound and draw arrows to indicate the jump-over pattern. For struggling learners, combining an oral and hands-on technique is often more effective than paper-and-pencil seatwork.

Occasionally, children might illustrate what is happening in a sentence, paying attention to the details (who? what? where?). This encourages them to attach meaning to the words they are reading.

Reuse sentence strips throughout the year for additional practice with the high-frequency words.

SENTENCES WITH HIGH-FREQUENCY WORDS

In these sentences the focus is on the italic words, which are taken from the indicated lists of high-frequency words (both decodable and look-at-and-know).

Reading Words from the A Lists

1. *We can help* Mom *make a* cake. *Here are the* pans.

2. *I can ride a* bike *to the big* hill. *You come, too.*

3. *Do you like the big blue* van?

4. Pick *up all the* balls *and run to me.*

5. *I am in a* box. *Can you jump in and play?*

6. *Some* trees *are tall and some* trees *are small.*

7. Did *you see the* dog? *He ran to look at the little* cat.

8. *Can you help me make a red* hat?

Reading Words from the B Lists

1. We *will always laugh* at a good joke.

2. *His* dog has *black* feet and a *brown* tail.

3. *Put* the vase *down or* it *may* fall.

4. Tom *said, "Let* Mom *buy* you the coat."

5. Call *her today if* you see *her* little dog here.

6. Help me *put away* the *three* pies we did not *eat.*

7. I *saw* you *draw* a *black* cat *for her.*

8. *Fly away,* little red and *black* bug!

Reading Words from the C Lists

1. *First,* you need to *open our new* box.

2. *Please* put *your* hand up *again.*

3. He saw *six* jets fly *over* the tops *of* the trees.

4. *Who made your funny green* kite?

5. She will *give ten* bones to her *five* dogs.

6. I can *read* for a *long* time on a cold day.

7. We *cut* up and *ate* the *four* cakes.

8. *Many of us wish* we *had new* bikes.

Reading Words from the D Lists

1. I *found* the *best white* stone.

2. Did *they ask about* the ten fish I have?

3. *Tell* me if *that* plant will *grow* to be tall.

4. Do you like to *sleep* in your *own* bed?

5. *This* train *only* goes *around* the track *once.*

6. We eat lots of green grapes *because they* are good.

7. *Thank* you so *much* for the pretty blue boat.

8. I will bake a pie *before they* go home.

Reading Words from the E Lists

1. Please write *both* of *their* names on the bag.

2. *Where* do you *want* me to put this *clean* glass?

3. The steam from the *warm* pot is *very* hot.

4. I *hurt* my leg *every* time I run too fast.

5. They can *pick* up *their* chairs because they are *very light.*

6. I *use* my *right* hand *when* I draw. *Which* hand do you *use?*

7. Did you know that *seven* comes *after eight?*

8. We *could* go to the show *together.*

Reading Confusable Words

1. Come to my home for some cake and milk. (*come, some*)

2. If you run fast, you could be in first place. (*fast, first*)

3. Here is her pretty white dress. (*here, her*)

4. A cold could make you very sick.   (*cold, could*)

5. Now I know how to tie my shoes.   (*now, know, how*)

6. Where were you when I came to see you?   (*where, were*)

7. The lake is very cold every day.   (*very, every*)

8. Did you say that you saw a dog and a cat?   (*say, saw*)

Which Word Is It?

Materials   Laminated sentence strips (see suggested sentences below); water-based markers

Present sentences from which you have omitted confusable high-frequency words. Maintain a controlled vocabulary, using only words that most children have mastered. Each sentence should include context clues to help children choose which of two confusable words makes sense in the blank. First, children circle the correct answer, then they write the word in the blank. Finally they read the sentence orally to be sure it makes sense.

When appropriate, ask children to act out the sentence, or to act out a situation in which someone might say the sentence; this helps them attach meaning to the words.

Sentences with Confusable Words Omitted

1. After you pet the dog, please _____ your hands.
   (**wish, wash**)

2. That cup is _____, so please do not spill it.
   (**full, fall**)

3. Do not _____ that red pen to write with.
   (**us, use**)

4. Who _____ this boy look like?
   (**goes, does**)

5. _____ many balls does Max have in the box?
   (**Now, How**)

6. The hen _____ seven chicks in her nest.
   (**was, has**)

7. You may go, _____ first wash your face.
   (put, **but**)

8. That man _____ on the boat with us.
   (saw, **was**)

9. I have to _____ my cat to the vet.
   (**take**, talk)

10. _____ do you want to go after the game?
    (Were, **Where**)

11. My mom and dad _____ to the lake.
    (when, **went**)

12. _____ ran together to the big pine tree.
    (Then, **They**)

HARD AND SOFT C AND G

PHONICS SKILL 9: Read words that have hard or soft *c* or *g*, knowing when to use each sound.

The first sounds children learn for *c* and *g* are their hard sounds: *c* as in *cat* and *g* as in *go*. However, sometimes *c* and *g* stand for other sounds; we pronounce soft *c* like the letter *s*, and soft *g* like the letter *j*.

These sounds are usually easy for children to remember because they hear them in the names of the letters, *cee* and *gee*. But which sound do they use when they find *c* or *g* in a new word? This is the general rule: *c* and *g* usually have their soft sounds when followed by *e*, *i*, or *y*. To master this skill, children need to focus on the letters that follow *c* and *g*.

Note that children don't need to know the terms *hard sound* and *soft sound*; what's important is knowing the two sounds for each letter.

In the general rule for this phonics skill, the words *followed by* sometimes confuse children. To help with this, have children touch the letters from left to right while you point out which letters *follow* or *come after* the *c* or *g*.

The Prove It! Game

Materials   Laminated cards for *c* and *g* words (prepare from lists below); highlighters; Which One Is It? chart

Distribute the word cards. On each card, the children highlight any *c* or *g* that is followed by *e, i,* or *y* and say the name of the letter as a trigger for the soft sound. Using highlighters keeps children actively involved and helps them focus on the letters that affect the sounds of *c* and *g*.

- Children take turns reading the words aloud.

- For each word, say to the reader, "Tell me how you know that word. Prove it." For example, a child who reads the word *nice* would explain that the *c* sounds like /s/ because it is followed by an *e*, and the *i* says its name because of the jump-over pattern.

- After "proving it," the child can write the word on the Which One Is It? chart.

- Continue until all the cards have been read.

This technique reinforces all the phonics skills previously taught.

HARD AND SOFT C AND G WORDS

Hard *c*	Soft *c*	Hard *g*	Soft *g*
can	cell	go	gee
cat	cent	got	gel
cup	face	gum	gem
clap	lace	glad	Gene
club	race	glass	age
crab	place	grab	cage
crib	space	grass	page
came	ice	green	stage
cane	mice	game	huge
coat	nice	gate	badge
cone	rice	hug	fudge
cube	price	rag	bridge
cute	slice	flag	
clean	twice		
cream	dance		
	fence		
	prince		

Reading C and G Words in Sentences

Materials	Laminated sentence strips (see suggested sentences below); water-based markers

For practice with encountering the *g* and *c* sounds in context, present sentences on laminated strips, using a controlled vocabulary. For each sentence, ask for volunteers to draw a box around any *c* or *g* and notice the following letter, then read the sentence aloud. You might also ask a child to act out the sentence to demonstrate understanding of its meaning.

Sentences with Hard and Soft C and G Words

1. If you run in the *race,* you *could* win first *place.*

2. The *ice cubes* make my drink very *cold!*

3. I will *cut* a *slice* of this *nice cake* for you.

4. Their three white *mice* have *cute* faces.

5. She put a *cup* of *rice* on a *clean* plate.

6. Just for today, the *price* of an *ice cream cone* is ten *cents.*

7. He used an old *rag* to wipe up the *cage.*

8. The *green gem* on her ring shines in the sun.

9. *Gene* likes to act funny on the *stage.*

10. The *goats* went over a little *bridge* and in the *gate.*

11. Write your name in *huge* print at the top of the *page.*

12. Can you tell the *age* of my *frog?*

◆ DAILY R-T-P ◆

Make word cards for words with hard and soft *c* and *g*. Hold up one word card at a time. Call on a volunteer to read the word, count the vowels, identify the pattern, and show you where the word belongs on the Which One Is It? chart.

Second Grade

Phonics, vocabulary building, and structural analysis skills give children the muscle they need to be powerful readers.

Children reading at the second-grade level continue to practice the phonics skills of first grade. At the same time, they add some spelling patterns to their repertoire that do not follow the rules taught to first graders, including many combinations of letters that do not sound the way they look. Some irregular spelling patterns appear more frequently than others, and we treat these as separate crucial skills. The irregular patterns that appear less frequently are grouped together.

- **Phonics Skill 10:** *R-controlled Vowels* In many simple words that look like a short-vowel pattern, the presence of *r* modifies the vowel sound. To remember this, children learn that the *r* makes the vowels "go crazy."

- **Phonics Skill 11: Words with *oo*** This letter combination has two sounds, which we help children remember with the trigger words *boo* and *book*.

- **Phonics Skill 12: Words with *ou* and *ow*** These letter combinations share the /ou/ diphthong sound; we call them "pinchy vowels" to help children make the connection with "ouch!" and "ow!"

- **Phonics Skill 13: Words with Long *i* and *o*** Counter to the one vowel, short sound pattern children have learned, the letter combination *igh* signals the long *i* sound. In addition, certain word endings, including *-nd, -ld, -lt, -st,* or *-ll,* may signal the long-vowel sound even though there is only one vowel (*i* or *o*).

- **Phonics Skill 14: Special Rule-Breaker Vowel Patterns** Several patterns break the first-grade rule that when we see two vowels together, the first says its name and the second is silent. Context clues are the key to helping children read words in these patterns: *ea* as in *bread, ei* as in *vein, ew* as in *few, ie* as in *field, oi* as in *boil, oy* as in *boy, aw* as in *saw, al* as in *ball, au* as in *fault,* and *augh* as in *taught.*

- **Phonics Skill 15: Unusual Consonant Combinations** Children learn to recognize the silent consonants in words that begin with *gn-, kn-,* and *wr-,* and to recognize that the combinations *ph* and *gh* sometimes signal the /f/ sound, as in *phone* and *laugh.*

Because these patterns are irregular, struggling readers need lots of practice with them. For this practice, we emphasize seeing new words in sentences so children can use context clues to supplement the phonics principles they are learning.

We also work on three vocabulary-building skills to increase reading fluency and to expand children's oral and written vocabularies.

- **Vocabulary Skill 2: Homophones** Children learn to distinguish between words that are pronounced the same but spelled differently and have different meanings.

- **Vocabulary Skill 3: Synonyms and Antonyms** Recognizing synonyms and their subtle differences in meaning and knowing common antonyms are skills that contribute to children's comprehension of what they are reading.

- **Vocabulary Skill 4: Multiple-Meaning Words** Prior experience with the definitions of words with several different meanings will help children recognize the right meaning when they come across such a word in story context.

By learning homophones, antonyms, synonyms, and words with multiple meanings, children build up a reserve of words that aid in increased comprehension. Again, the emphasis is on using words in context and asking children to "see" what they are reading as they work toward the larger goal— to gain meaning from print.

Structural analysis is another major focus at the second-grade reading level. When children learn to break down large words into smaller words or word parts, the decoding is simplified: now they can use what they know to figure out what they don't know. We teach six skills in structural analysis.

- **Structural Skill 1: Compound Words** To read a compound word, children look for the two smaller words that were put together.

- **Structural Skill 2: Contractions** Another form of two words put together is the contraction, in which an apostrophe takes the place of one or more letters.

- **Structural Skill 3: Spelling Changes with Common Suffixes** The plural endings -s and -es, the verb endings -ing and -ed, and the comparative endings -er and -est are all part of children's oral vocabularies, and many will read them without difficulty at the second-grade level.

  However, there are some potential problems when spelling changes occur: doubling the final consonant, dropping the silent e, or changing a final y to an i. An analysis of these patterns helps children in both their reading and their writing.

- **Structural Skill 4: Long-Word Decoding** With simple "help cards," we give children a specific code that helps them break up longer, more difficult words by identifying common spelling patterns. They then read each part and put all the parts together to say the word.

- **Structural Skill 5: Prefixes *un-* and *re-*** Through word-building activities, children learn to identify root words and two common prefixes that change their meaning.

- **Structural Skill 6: Suffixes *-ful, -y, -less,* and *-ly*** Children learn to identify four common suffixes that change the function of root words—from nouns to adjectives, or from adjectives to adverbs.

For struggling learners, quick daily reviews are critical for mastery. If children have not mastered first-grade phonics skills, continue to use the teaching tool Which One Is It? (p. 22). In addition, you will need to begin daily review of the new second-grade skills, continuing to use the R-T-P format (review, teach or reteach skills, then practice).

The teaching tool for review of second-grade skills is the Reading Tools chart of thirteen boxes (p. 49). You can either present this chart all at once, or build it over time by adding a new "box" each time you teach one of the specific skills.

- The first row reviews the short- and long-vowel patterns taught as first-grade skills.

- The second row focuses on the most common irregular vowel spelling patterns taught as second-grade skills.

- The third row reviews contractions and their spelling patterns.

- The fourth row reviews types of spelling changes that take place when we add common endings to root words.

- The final row reviews other ways good readers figure out unknown words: by breaking up longer words into smaller parts, as suggested by the long word help card; by looking for root words; and by using surrounding words for clues.

Children use the Reading Tools chart for reference, categorizing words according to the boxes. The chart is especially useful for daily R-T-P.

Reading Tools

one vowel	two vowels together	_____ e
r makes vowels go crazy. ar, er, ir, or, ur	oo → boo oo → book	ou → out ow → cow

Contractions

I am	(I'm)	we have	(we've)
he is	(he's)	you would	(you'd)
we are	(we're)	is not	(isn't)
she will	(she'll)	let us	(let's)

Double the final consonant. hopping hopped sadder saddest	Drop silent e. baking baked safer safest	y → i bunny bunnies funny funniest
Use the long-word help card.	Look at the root word.	Look at the other words for clues.

R-CONTROLLED VOWELS

PHONICS SKILL 10: Read words with *r*-controlled vowels
(*ar, or, er, ir, ur*).

Words with *r*-controlled vowels introduce an irregular spelling pattern. That is, children first learned that when they count one vowel in a word, it has the short vowel sound. But when the vowel is followed by *r*, that rule no longer works; the vowel sound with an *r* is neither short nor long. We tell children that an *r* makes vowels "go crazy." This helps them focus on the vowel-*r* combination and its special sound.

Teaching the Sounds of Vowels with R

Materials Resource lists of words with *r*-controlled vowels (p. 52)

Begin with an oral drill of the five sounds of *r*-controlled vowels. For example:

- Write the combination *ar* on the board and state, "a-r says . . ." The children respond by saying the sound of *ar* (as in *art*).

- Next write *or* and say, "o-r says . . ." The children respond by saying the sound of *or* (as in *for*).

- Finally write *er, ir,* and *ur,* and say, "e-r, i-r, and u-r all say . . ." The children respond by saying the *er* sound (as in *her, first,* and *turn*).

Oral exercises help auditory learners. For children who are struggling with the sounds, you might teach them the trigger words *art, for, her, first,* and *turn.*

To reverse the process to a written drill, give the children one sound at a time to write on their papers. Ask them to spell the *ar* sound, then to write the *or* sound, and finally to show three ways to write the *er* sound.

These written exercises help visual and kinesthetic learners. Oral and written exercises together help lock *r*-controlled spelling patterns and sounds in children's minds.

R-controlled Vowels in Words

Materials Laminated lists of words with r-controlled vowels (prepare from lists, p. 52); highlighters or water-based markers

At the first-grade level, we taught children to box the letters that stand for one sound. They can use this same technique to link the vowel and the *r* that changes the vowel sound.

In each word on their lists, children draw a box around the vowel and the following *r*. Alternatively, they can use highlighters on the letters. Then when you say, "What letters jump out at you in that word?" they clearly see the two letters together in the spelling pattern. Once children recognize that two letters connect to make one sound, they usually read the whole word without difficulty.

R-controlled Vowels: Reading for Meaning

Materials   Laminated lists of words with *r*-controlled vowels (prepare from lists, p. 52); strips of colored paper; water-based markers

Provide sheets of words with *r*-controlled vowels listed in columns and have children place their strips of colored paper under the first line of *ar, or, er, ir,* and *ur* words. The strips help struggling readers focus on one line of words at a time.

Choose one word from the list and give a clue related to its meaning. For example, "Find the word that means you are talking about a girl." Children use water-based markers and circle the word that fits your clue (in this case, *her*).

ar	or	er	ir	ur
art	for	(her)	first	turn
car	cork	fern	girl	burn
farm	forth	germ	sir	curb

Continue in this way, having children slide their strips down to each successive line of words as you call out clues that connect meaning to selected words. Check for understanding by looking to see that children have circled the correct words.

Reading Words with R-controlled Vowels in Sentences

Materials   Laminated sentence strips (see suggested sentences, p. 53); water-based markers or highlighters

Prepare laminated sentence strips from the examples given. These sentences have a controlled vocabulary; in addition to the words with *r*-controlled vowels (italicized), they use only words with familiar short- and long-vowel patterns and words from the high-frequency lists. Using a controlled vocabulary guarantees success for children because it builds on their strengths. In addition, it provides a review of all previously learned skills.

Have children read the sentence strips orally. Before they read, allow them to scan the print and use water-based markers or highlighters to box letters that go together, draw arrows to indicate "jump-over" long-vowel patterns, or accent certain letters. As needed, remind them of the trigger words for *r*-controlled sounds: *art, for, her, first,* and *turn.*

As a check for meaning, ask children to illustrate a sentence, being sure to show the details. Alternatively, some struggling readers enjoy shining penlights on the specific words in a sentence that answer questions about details (who? what? when? where?).

WORDS WITH *R*-CONTROLLED VOWELS

ar	*or*	*er*	*ir*	*ur*
art	for	her	first	turn
car	fork	Bert	bird	fur
card	cork	fern	girl	burn
farm	forth	germ	sir	curb
park	fort	herd	dirt	curl
yard	horn	jerk	stir	hurt
bark	born	nerve	fir	nurse
arm	stork	perch	shirt	purse
star	porch	clerk	skirt	church
dark	more	verse	third	curve
hard	tore	serve	twirl	burr
jar	before	were	whirl	purr
march	corn	stern	squirt	burst
shark	storm	better	thirst	spurs
chart	sports	under	squirm	purple
Mark	store	over	birch	hurry
sharp	thorn	verb	chirp	further
smart	horse	after	birthday	churn
yarn	short	swerve	swirl	surprise

Sentences with R-controlled Vowels

1. Stand on the *curb* and look both ways *before* you cross the street.

2. The grass in *her yard* is so green, it is like a *park*.

3. My dog dug a hole in the *dirt under* the *porch*.

4. You *are* not the *first* in line. You will be *third*.

5. When we get to the *farm,* we will *park* the *car* next to the *barn*.

6. The *shark* has *sharp* teeth. If a *shark* bites you, it will *hurt*.

7. *Mark* broke his left *arm* when he fell off his bike.

8. When you *turn* on the stove, try not to *burn* your hand.

9. A pretty red *bird* sat on a *perch* in the cage.

10. Will he buy *more corn* when he goes to the *store?*

WORDS WITH OO

PHONICS SKILL 11: Read words with *oo* pronounced with a long-vowel sound as in *boo* and a short-vowel sound as in *book*.

Words that have the *oo* spelling pattern do not follow the "two vowels together" pattern taught as a first-grade skill. We teach children trigger words to associate with the two different sounds of *oo*, /uw/ as in *boo* and /u/ as in *book*. These words (*boo* and *book*) are easily remembered because they look very similar. After teaching the new sounds, asking "Does *oo* ever say the long *o* sound?" reminds children that this combination of letters breaks the rules, just as the *r*-controlled vowels did.

Teaching the OO Vowel Sounds

Materials   Resource lists for words with *oo* (p. 54); paper and pencil

Use this visual and kinesthetic technique to teach and practice the two *oo* vowel sounds. When you name one of the sounds and a word containing that sound, children write the letters and the trigger word for that sound. For example:

You say:	Children write:
"Write the /oo/ sound as in *spoon*."	*oo* as in *boo*
"Spell the /oo/ sound as in *hook*."	*oo* as in *book*

Continue with other examples from the word list. If the children write a single *o*, ask, "What does one *o* say?" This prompts children to recall the first-grade rule about words with one vowel, and the hand motion that triggers the short *o* as in *on the desk* (placing one hand, fingertips down, on the desk). Use any such mistakes to reinforce the difference between the short-vowel and long-vowel spelling patterns and the new irregular-vowel spelling patterns.

WORDS WITH OO

/uw/ as in *boo*		/u/ as in *book*	
boo	soon	book	good
boot	tool	foot	soot
room	spoon	cook	hood
hoop	stool	hook	took
food	tooth	wool	look
moon	broom	stood	wood
noon	cool	brook	
pool	goose	shook	

A Spelling Game for OO Words

Materials   Resource list for words with *oo* (above); paper and pencil

Children fold a sheet of paper in half. At the top of the two sections they write "*oo* as in boo" and "*oo* as in book."

As you call out words from the *oo* lists, children echo the word you said, listen to the sound of *oo* in that word, and write the word under the correct heading. For example:

- Call out the word *hook*.

- Children echo the word aloud, then think, "When I say *hook*, I hear *oo* as in *book*."

- Children then write the word *hook* on their papers under the "*oo* as in book" heading.

At the end of this activity, have children read orally all the words on their papers.

Variation: Using Word-Meaning Clues To weave comprehension with phonics instruction, give word clues instead of the words themselves. For example:

- You say: "Write the name of a place where you can swim."

- Children think: "A place where you can swim is a pool. When I say *pool*, I hear *oo* as in *boo*."

- Children write the word *pool* under the correct heading on their papers.

Again, when the game is over, have children read all the *oo* words they have written.

Reading OO Words in Sentences

Materials	Laminated sentence strips (see suggested sentences below); water-based markers or highlighters; paper and pencil or crayons

Present sentences that use a controlled vocabulary and *oo* words. In unison, children read the sentence aloud as you rhythmically tap under each word. Children might touch the words themselves as they read to the rhythmic beat of the teacher's tapping.

Use this unison reading as a chance to identify the weaknesses of your struggling learners; noting any gaps in learning assists in your planning of daily R-T-P practice. Continued use of kinesthetic and visual techniques—boxing in letters, highlighting letters that make one sound, and asking, "What jumps out at you?"—helps children focus on the short-vowel, long-vowel, and irregular spelling patterns.

After children finish reading a sentence, have them recall and possibly illustrate the literal details of what they have read: who is in the sentence, what they are doing, where they are, and when the action takes place.

Not every sentence will have the same types of details, and not all details are easily drawn. However, writing the questions *who? what? when? where?* on the board and asking children to tell you about or illustrate as many of these as they can helps them focus on reading the sentences for meaning.

Sentences with OO Words

1. Mom *took* the *wool* coat off the *hook* and gave it to Mark.

2. My *tooth* is *loose*, and I hope it will fall out *soon*.

3. On hot days we can *cool* off with a swim in the *pool.*

4. We saw two pigs, six hens, a *goose,* and a horse on the farm.

5. On very cold days, I pull up my *hood* to keep warm.

6. Put a sock on your *foot* before you put on your *boot.*

7. At *noon,* Mom will *cook* eggs and toast for our lunch.

8. Tom and Glen *took* us to the *zoo* to see the apes.

9. Please get the *broom* so we can sweep the *room.*

10. My dad keeps many *tools* in his large *tool* chest.

WORDS WITH OU AND OW

PHONICS SKILL 12: Read words with *ou* and *ow* pronounced as in *out* and *cow.*

Words with *ou* and *ow* represent two more irregular-spelling patterns. That is, words with *ou,* such as *out,* don't follow the "two vowels together" rule, and words with *ow,* such as *cow,* don't follow the "one vowel, short sound" rule. We introduce the term "pinchy vowels" as a mnemonic aid that helps children remember both spellings for this new sound.

WORDS WITH *OU*			WORDS WITH *OW*		
out	noun	around	cow	owl	frown
cloud	found	ground	how	bow-wow	growl
loud	proud	round	now	clown	power
house	about	sound	bow	brown	tower
mouse	trout	pound	down	crown	flower
blouse	south	pounce	town	drown	vowels

Teaching the Pinchy Vowel Sounds

Materials   Resource lists for words with *ou* and *ow* (above)

Write the words *out* and *cow* on the board. Read the words and call on children to box the letters that have the "ow" sound.

Explain that you are going to call these "pinchy vowels" because when someone pinches us, we say "ow!" or "ouch!" In these words, we hear the "ow!" sound of *ou* and *ow*. Show the children how to make a pinching motion with their fingers. The pinchy vowel device is fun for children and gets them actively involved.

The trigger words *out* and *cow*, which most children spell easily, can also help them recall both spellings. Asking "Does *ou* ever say the long *o* sound?" reminds children that this combination of letters breaks the "two-vowels together" rule.

Teaching the Long O Sound for OW

Materials   Resource list of words in which *ow* has the long *o* sound (below)

In another irregular spelling pattern, *ow* sometimes represents the long *o* sound, as in *snow*. There are enough common words in this pattern that children need to be aware of it. Several words in this pattern are familiar to children from the high-frequency word lists: *grow, know, own, show,* and *yellow*.

When children encounter an unknown *ow* word in their reading, there is no way to tell just by looking at the letters whether they should use the "pinchy" sound or the long *o* sound. In these cases, children need to try both pronunciations and use context clues to make sense of what they are reading.

Because context clues are critical for proper decoding, present these long *o* words only in phrases, such as *what do you know, the wind blows, the cold snow,* and *cars in the slow lane*. Help children focus on the choice they must make by asking if the "pinchy" sound would make sense.

WORDS WITH OW AND THE LONG O SOUND		
grow	blow	row
know	flow	bowl
own	glow	throw
show	crow	mow
yellow	slow	mower
snow	low	known

Reading OU and OW Words in Sentences

Materials   Laminated lists of sentences with *ou* and *ow* words (prepare from lists, pp. 58–59); water-based markers and highlighters

On the first list, ask children to read each sentence aloud, in unison. To help them focus on the print, children should be touching, saying, and hearing the words as they read orally. This process combines visual, auditory, and kinesthetic modalities. It helps struggling learners because, unlike when they read solo, they are not singled out.

Note that using context clues can help children distinguish between words with *ow* as in *cow* and long *o* as in *snow*. Encourage them to box or highlight letters that make one sound.

In the sentences on the second list, the *ou* and *ow* words have been omitted. Children use context clues and active thinking (thinking about what the words mean and picturing them in their minds) to fill in the blanks with words from the word bank (p. 59).

Sentences with OU and OW Words

1. After you sing and dance, take a bow and wave to the crowd.

2. An owl is a bird, and a trout is a fish.

3. Please don't shout, because loud sounds hurt my ears.

4. A dog says bow-wow, but a cat says meow.

5. We saw a brown cow when we spent the day on a farm.

6. Is that a smile or a frown on your face?

7. When I am at bat, I hate to strike out or hit a foul ball.

8. If you fall into a deep lake and you do not know how to swim, you may drown.

9. The owl hunts in the dark. She would like to catch a mouse.

10. If you act like a grouch, no one will like you.

11. Some birds fly south when the days turn cold in the fall.

12. The sun is like a big, round, yellow ball in the sky.

13. That town is very small. It has only three stores.

14. The rain makes the pretty flowers grow tall.

15. Bring a broom and help me clean the house.

Fill-in Sentences with OU and OW Words

1. The hat for a king or queen is known as a _____.

2. I like to fish from a boat. I try to catch _____.

3. To plant a tree, first we dig a hole in the _____.

4. When it rains, we see many dark _____ in the sky.

5. The milk that we drink comes from _____.

6. If you tease that dog, he may _____ at you.

7. Liz wore a red skirt and a white _____.

8. The _____ did funny tricks and made us laugh.

9. When the bell rings, it makes a very loud _____.

10. We rode our sleds _____ the hill in the snow.

WORD BANK				
clown	crown	cows	down	growl
clouds	blouse	ground	sound	trout

Cumulative Practice with Irregular-Vowel Spelling Patterns

Materials Laminated sets of six index cards, with irregular-vowel spelling patterns as shown (one set per child); water-based markers; blank index cards, laminated and taped together in strips (for variation)

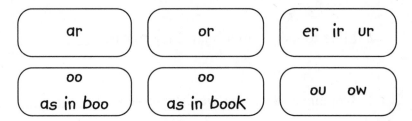

Have children lay out their cards faceup in front of them. Say the sound on one of the cards. Children repeat the sound and pick up the card that has the corresponding spelling. For example:

- You say, "*ow* as in *couch*."
- Children repeat "*ow*" and pick up the card with *ou* and *ow*.

After repeated practices like this, reverse the procedure. Now you hold up a card with an irregular-vowel spelling pattern on it, and the children say its sound.

Variation: Relating Sounds and Spellings Say a word that contains one of the irregular-vowel spelling patterns. Children repeat the word, touch the card that shows the spelling pattern they hear, then flip the card over and write the word with water-based markers. Write the word on the board so children are able to check their work, and, if necessary, make corrections.

Variation: Spelling Strips Give each child a connected strip of six laminated, blank index cards. They must be able to fold the strip to show anywhere from one to six cards at a time. Say a word with one of the irregular-vowel spelling patterns and tell children how many letters are in the word (no more than six letters). Children unfold their strips to show one blank card for each letter in the word. They repeat the word and think about how the word is spelled, then use water-based markers to write the word, one letter on each card. Check their work and ask them to make any needed corrections.

• DAILY R-T-P •

Review short-vowel, long-vowel, and irregular-vowel spelling patterns with the first two rows on the Reading Tools wall chart. Pointing to the boxes in turn, ask students what they mean.

When reviewing the skills of the first three boxes, encourage children to get actively involved by using the hand motions they learned: holding up either one finger (short vowels), two fingers together (double long-vowel pattern), or a thumb up (jump-over pattern).

- For "one vowel," children should be able to tell you that one vowel in a word has the short sound.
- For "two vowels together," children should be able to tell you that the first vowel says its name and the second one is silent.
- For the "jump-over" pattern, Children should know that the *e* jumps over the consonant to the first vowel and makes that vowel say its name.

As children read words for practice, encourage them to highlight the patterns by boxing letters that make one sound and drawing arrows.

• DAILY R-T-P •

Use the second row of boxes on the Reading Tools wall chart to review irregular-vowel spelling patterns. Children should be reminded that these patterns "break the rules" of the first row.

- Children should be able to tell you what we mean when we say "*r* makes vowels go crazy."
- They should know the three sounds of *r*-controlled vowels.
- They should know the two sounds of *oo* (as in *boo* and *book*).
- They should know the "pinchy vowel" sound for *ou* as in *out* and *ow* as in *cow*.

WORDS WITH LONG I AND O

PHONICS SKILL 13: Read words with long *i* spelled *igh* as in *light,* and words in which *i* and *o* have the long sound before certain special endings (*-nd, -ld, -ll, -lt, -lk, st*).

Children have previously learned two patterns for spelling the long *i* and long *o* sounds: two vowels together (as in *pie* and *boat*), and the jump-over pattern (as in *like* and *home*). Now they learn some irregular spellings for the same sounds.

- Children learn that the long *i* sound can be spelled *igh* as in *light* and come to recognize this group of letters as having one sound.

- They also learn another exception to the one-vowel, short-sound rule: Words with one *i* or one *o* and certain special endings may have the long vowel sound. These endings include *-nd* (*find*), *-ld* (*wild, gold*), *-ll* (*roll*), *-lt* (*colt*), *-lk* (*folk*), and *-st* (*most*).

WORDS WITH LONG *I* SPELLED *IGH*

right	night	bright
sigh	fight	flight
light	tight	might
fright	sight	tonight
high	slight	

LONG *I* AND LONG *O* WORDS WITH SPECIAL ENDINGS

find	wild	old	roll	colt
kind	mild	gold	toll	bolt
mind	child	told	troll	jolt
blind		sold	stroll	
grind		hold		most
wind		cold		post
		fold		
		scold		folk
				yolk

Practicing Irregular Spelling Patterns for Long I and O

Materials   Lists of words with irregular spellings for long *i* and long *o*, posted on chart paper (prepare from lists, p. 62)

Direct a quick, oral practice of words with irregular long *i* and long *o* spelling patterns, using posted word lists. As you point to a word, children read it orally. This practice helps children visually recognize and pronounce these words.

To connect meaning to the words, give oral clues and ask children to find the word you are thinking of on the posted lists. For example:

- You say: "The opposite of *low* is . . ."
- Looking at the posted lists, children say and write the word *high*.

Continue giving oral clues until you have practiced all the words on the lists. To call attention to the silent *gh* in the *igh* pattern, have children box the letters that have a single sound (*igh*) and cross out the letters that are silent (*gh*).

Reading Irregular Long I and Long O Words in Sentences

Materials   Laminated sentence strips (see suggested sentences, pp. 64–65); catchers' mitts cut from poster board, with a rectangular space cut in the center, then laminated

During your usual practice with oral reading of sentences, give the children laminated catchers' mitts. This kinesthetic technique helps children practice active thinking, as they create mental images of the words they are reading.

Before children begin to read each new sentence, tell them to "catch" a particular word. To "catch" a word, they locate it in the window of their mitt. For example, they might catch the word that tells *who* or *what* is doing something in the sentence, a word that tells *what* is being done, or a word that tells *where* it is happening.

To connect meaning to the new words, give meaning clues, telling children, for example, to "catch" the word in the sentence that names a baby horse (*colt*).

We suggest using both complete sentences for oral reading and sentences that require children to fill in the blanks. All use a controlled vocabulary so children are practicing only skills that have been previously taught, in addition to the new irregular spellings of long *i* and long *o* words.

Sentences with Long I Spelled IGH

1. The owl is a bird that likes to hunt at *night*.

2. The old house stood at the top of a *high* hill.

3. Do you write with your left hand or your *right* hand?

4. His new shirt did not fit because it was too *tight*.

5. Turn off the *light* when you go to bed.

6. The man drove a *bright* red sports car.

7. Our cat always *fights* with our dog.

8. Come out *tonight* and look at the stars.

Sentences with Long I and Long O Before Special Endings

1. Kate likes to *hold* her cat and pet him.

2. When it got dark, my dad *told* me to go to bed.

3. Take a warm coat because it is very *cold* today.

4. Do you think Max will *mind* if we use his bike?

5. To drive over the *toll* bridge, we must pay a *toll*.

6. An egg has a yellow *yolk*.

7. We must be *kind* to all of our pets.

8. I *sold* my *old* bike to the *child* down the street.

9. She hopes she can *find* the ring that she lost.

10. The *blind* man walks down the street with a white cane.

Fill-In Sentences with Long I and Long O Words

1. I have to keep my new pants clean or my mom will _____ me.
   (hold, scold)

2. On a _____ spring day, the sun feels warm on my face.
   (child, mild)

3. I would like to have a ring made of _____.
   (cold, gold)

4. When we do the wash at home, I help _____ my clean shirts.
   (fold, told)

5. My dog ran away. Can you help me _____ him?
   (find, kind)

6. We had a _____ storm with lots of cold rain and big winds.
   (mind, wild)

7. There is an old _____ tale about a troll who lives under a
   bridge.   (yolk, folk)

8. Max is a nice _____ who says "please" and "thank you."
   (colt, child)

9. My dog is very smart because he knows how to _____ over.
   (roll, toll)

10. The pretty brown horse is in the barn with her new _____.
    (jolt, colt)

11. Do you _____ if I sit with you while I eat my lunch?
    (mind, mild)

12. We put a house for a bird on the top of a tall _____.
    (most, post)

SPECIAL RULE-BREAKER VOWEL PATTERNS

PHONICS SKILL 14: Read words with special rule-breaker vowel patterns (*ea, ei, ew, oi, oy, aw, al, au, augh*).

Children are taught as a first-grade pattern that a word with two vowels together has the long sound of the first vowel. Now, they learn a number of exceptions to this rule. We treat these special rule-breaker patterns together as one skill, and we emphasize helping children use context clues to correctly read the new words.

We suggest daily, guided, oral and written practice sessions that connect meaning to the words, whether they are presented in isolation (on lists) or in sentences, so children learn them through active thinking rather than through memorization.

Connecting Meaning to Special Rule-Breaker Words

Materials   Lists of words with rule-breaker vowel patterns, posted on chart paper (prepare from lists, p. 67); paper and pencil

Play a game of "Which word am I thinking of?" to help children read these new words and connect meaning to them. Practice each list of words separately.

Tell children the number of letters in the word you are thinking of, and give them oral clues about its meaning. On their paper, children draw short blanks for each letter in the word, think about the clues given, and write the word, putting one letter in each blank. For example:

- You say: "I am thinking of a word on the *e-a* as in *bread* list. My word has four letters. Here is the clue. The word means the part of your body that includes your brain. Write the word."

- Children write the word *head*.

When you have asked about every word on the "*ea* as in *bread*" list, have children orally read the words they have written.

Play this game with each of the ten lists of words. In these lists, children encounter two more patterns, similar to *igh* as in *light,* in which the *gh* is silent: the *weigh, sleigh* family, and the *taught, caught* family. You might have children box the letters that make one sound in these words (*eigh* or *augh*) and cross out the letters that are silent.

WORDS WITH SPECIAL RULE-BREAKER VOWEL PATTERNS

ea as in *bread*	*ei* as in *vein*	*ew* as in *new*	*ie* as in *field*
bread	vein	new	field
dead	reins	dew	shield
deaf	veil	chew	piece
head	beige	drew	niece
read	weigh	grew	chief
thread	sleigh	blew	brief
breath	eight	flew	grief
feather	weight	stew	thief
leather	freight	knew	shriek
weather		threw	

oy as in *boy*		*oi* as in *oil*	
boy	soy	oil	voice
joy	royal	boil	choice
toy	loyal	soil	noise
		spoil	moist
		coin	point
		join	joint

aw as in *saw*	*al* as in *ball*	*au* as in *fault*	*augh* as in *taught*
saw	ball	fault	taught
paw	call	haul	caught
jaw	fall	pause	naughty
law	hall	cause	daughter
claw	mall	gauze	
draw	tall	sauce	
straw	wall	haunt	
dawn	small		
fawn	talk		
yawn	walk		
hawk	chalk		
crawl	salt		
	false		

Reading Special Rule-Breaker Words in Sentences

Materials Laminated sentence strips (see suggested sentences below); water-based markers or highlighters

Sentences with a controlled vocabulary and many context clues help children actively think about what the words mean and picture them in their minds. As they orally read the sentences, they may mark any spelling patterns and circle or highlight context clues.

In fill-in-the-blank sentences, children circle the correct word and write it in the blank. In sentences without blanks, ask children to orally give the meaning of those words with special rule-breaker patterns.

Children sometimes confuse similar-looking words like *walk* and *wake*, or *talk* and *take*. Showing the words together in context helps children discriminate between them. For example, present sentences like these:

- When you *wake* up from your nap, *walk* to the park with me.

- *Take* my hand and *talk* to me about what you'll be when you grow up.

Another way to emphasize the difference is to have children draw the arrow for the jump-over pattern in words with silent *e*.

Sentences with EA

1. We went to the store to get a loaf of _____ and jam.
(**breath, bread**)

2. If you rip your shirt, you need some _____ to stitch it up again. (**thread, bread**)

3. The king and queen both have gold crowns on their _____.
(**heads, threads**)

4. She made a tall stack of all the books she has _____ this year. (**dead, read**)

5. When it is cold, you can see your _____ as white clouds in the air. (**bread, breath**)

6. The clown had blue hair and a funny hat on his _____.
   (head, bread)

7. A green leaf turns brown when it is _____.
   (dead, bread)

8. We found a blue _____ that a bird had lost.
   (leather, feather)

Sentences with EI

1. The bride wore a long white dress and a *veil* over her face.

2. We had to stop our car at the tracks and wait for the *freight* train to go by.

3. When you ride a horse, pull on the *reins* to make the horse turn left or right.

4. A word that means light brown is *beige*.

5. Step on the scales to see how much you *weigh*.

6. When you are in third grade, you are about *eight* years old.

Sentences with EW

1. When the sun rose, the grass was wet with *dew*.

2. The owl *flew* into a tall pine tree and gave two hoots.

3. We saw only a *few* little fish in the stream, all too small to catch.

4. I *blew* my nose many times when I had a cold.

5. He *threw* the ball up at the hoop, but it hit the rim.

6. Would you like a stick of gum to *chew?*

Sentences with IE

1. The boys go to play ball down at the _____.
   (chief, field)

2. If you steal my piece of pie, I will call you a _____.
                                            (thief, brief)

3. Your speech should not be too long. Keep it _____.
                                            (shriek, brief)

4. Please cut me a small _____ of cake.
                         (piece, field)

5. The fire _____ is in charge of those who fight fires.
            (chief, thief)

6. If you scare me, I may let out a big _____.
                                        (piece, shriek)

Sentences with OI and OY

1. Please keep your *voice* down. You are too loud.

2. Would you like to *join* the *Boy* Scouts?

3. A pin has a sharp *point* that can poke you.

4. My dad always checks the *oil* in the car before we take a trip.

5. They took me to the *toy* store to look at a train.

6. We need to eat that fish before it *spoils*.

Sentences with AW, AL, AU, and AUGH

1. The cook put *salt* and pepper on the eggs to make them taste better.

2. When you *walk* on ice, try not to *fall* down.

3. I must *walk* the horse back to its *stall* in the barn so I can brush it.

4. If you look at me next to my dad, he is *tall* and I am short.

5. Who *taught* you how to read so well?

6. I threw the ball and he *caught* it in his mitt.

7. We have to mow the *lawn* every week so the grass does not get too long.

8. If you say "Shake," my dog will give you his *paw*.

Unusual Consonant Combinations

PHONICS SKILL 15: Read words with initial silent letters (*gn-*, *kn-*, *wr-*) and words in which *ph* and *gh* signal the /f/ sound.

Children learn to read common consonant blends and digraphs as a first-grade skill. Now, we present three pairs of consonants that have a silent letter and thus have a single sound instead of a blend, plus two digraphs that sound very different from the way they look.

All of these consonant combinations are somewhat uncommon. That is, in reading materials at a second-grade level, children will rarely encounter *gn* as in *gnaw*. They do, however, already know some high-frequency words with the silent-letter combinations *kn* as in *know* and *wr* as in *write*. They can now identify these silent consonants as a pattern that also appears in other words.

In each of the three pairs (*gn, kn, wr*), the first letter is silent and the second one has the usual consonant sound. The rest of the word can be easily read with phonics patterns the children have already learned: the one-vowel, short-sound pattern in *gnat,* the jump-over pattern in *write,* two-vowels-together in *kneel,* and so forth.

The new digraphs, *ph* as in *phone* and *gh* as in *laugh,* both have the /f/ sound, even though the letter *f* does not appear in the word. Again, these patterns appear relatively infrequently in reading materials at the second-grade level.

Many of the *ph* words, in particular, are multisyllabic, and you might want to help children with long-word decoding (Structural Skill 4) before presenting this list. Still, the list includes words that are both familiar and fun for the children (*elephant, alphabet*), and they usually enjoy learning the "silly" sound of /f/ for the letters *ph*.

The *-gh* words present another difficulty for struggling readers, because the *ou* takes on different vowel sounds from word to word: short *o* as in *cough,* short *u* as in *rough*. Furthermore, the *ough* pattern in which the *gh* has the /f/ sound is indistinguishable in print from the pattern in which the *gh* is silent (*though, through, bought*).

WORDS WITH SILENT INITIAL LETTERS

gn	*kn*	*wr*
gnaw	know	wrap
gnash	knock	wren
gnat	knit	wreck
gnome	knife	wring
gnu	knead	wrong
	kneel	wreath
	knew	write
	knot	wrench
	knee	wrist
	knight	wrote
	knob	

WORDS WITH /F/ SPELLED *PH* OR *GH*

ph		*gh*
phone	dolphin	laugh
photo	elephant	cough
graph	telephone	trough
phonics	alphabet	tough
phrase	gopher	rough
paragraph	autograph	enough

When children encounter an *-ough* word in their reading, they may need to try out all the different patterns and rely on context clues to help them recognize which pronunciation is called for in that particular case.

Teaching Words with Unusual Consonant Combinations

Materials   Laminated lists of words for each unusual consonant pattern (prepare from lists above); water-based markers or highlighters

An oral technique for familiarizing children with the pronunciation of these unusual words is to "echo read" each list, as follows:

• Pass out a list for each word group.

- To introduce the list, explain which letter is silent, or which two letters sound like the letter *f*.

- Read the first word on the list.

- The children echo you to practice the correct pronunciation.

- Continue with echo reading until children have read the entire list.

If children are having difficulty, remind them to use phonics skills they have learned previously. They can use water-based markers or highlighters to help them focus on the patterns they recognize, drawing an arrow for the jump-over pattern, boxing two letters that make one sound, and so forth.

Establishing Meaning for Words with Unusual Consonant Combinations

Materials   Laminated lists of words for each unusual consonant pattern (prepare from lists, p. 72)

Many of the words in these lists may be unfamiliar to children. If they are not already in children's oral vocabularies, they will be difficult to read.

For successful reading, we must help children link their prior experience to the new words. For example, to teach the word *gnaw,* we can link it to the familiar word *chew,* and explain that we often use the word *gnaw* when we talk about animals chewing. That is, we may say that dogs and lions *gnaw* on bones, or that a mouse *gnaws* a hole in the wall, or that beavers *gnaw* on tree trunks and branches.

You can also help establish meaning for these words through role-playing. With their understanding of the link between *chew* and *gnaw,* children can role-play a dog gnawing on a bone. What they know about the word *chew* helps them remember and understand the meaning of the word *gnaw.*

While children are reading orally through the lists of words, make meaning links and use role-playing as often as necessary. This technique increases children's vocabularies.

If children are already familiar with synonyms (Vocabulary Skill 3), they might brainstorm and write lists of synonyms for the new words.

Reading Words with Unusual Consonant Combinations in Sentences

Materials   Laminated sentence strips (see suggested sentences below)

When children are reading sentences that contain words with initial silent letters (*gn, kn, wr*) and words with the digraphs *ph* and *gh,* you will see three overlapping components of reading instruction at work: phonics, vocabulary building, and comprehension.

Knowledge of phonics skills helps children pronounce the words. Your work to establish prior knowledge of the unknown words entailed vocabulary building. These two components, used in conjunction with comprehension of context clues, enable children to understand what they read.

As children orally read the sentences, others role-play or illustrate what the sentences tell them. For example, consider the sentence, "The dog likes to gnaw on the bone because it tastes good." The context clues *dog, bone,* and *taste* help children understand the meaning of the new word *gnaw.*

Sentences for Words with Unusual Consonant Combinations

1. The little dog likes to *gnaw* on the bone because it tastes good.

2. The man who sells brooms came up the steps to *knock* on our door.

3. Our car has a big dent in the side because it was in a *wreck.*

4. When a pipe under the sink sprang a leak, my dad fixed it with a *wrench.*

5. I have a *photo* of Michael Jordan with his *autograph* on it.

6. Sue told a funny joke that made me *laugh.*

7. *Gnats* are little bugs that are pests. They fly in your face, and some may bite you.

8. Tom woke up with a cold and a bad *cough,* so he went back to bed.

9. My grandmother *knows* how to *knit* a sweater for me.

10. When you *wring* water out of a washcloth, you twist it with your *wrists.*

11. My sister likes to talk on the *phone* all day and all night.

12. I got to pet an *elephant* at the zoo, and his skin felt very *rough.*

HOMOPHONES

Children do not always know that the different spellings of homophones also indicate different meanings. Struggling learners tend to assume that when words sound the same (*blue, blew*), they also have the same meaning. These readers are only hearing words and are not connecting them to print.

To eliminate this confusion, we use both auditory and visual methods, in conjunction with context clues, to teach homophones. The visual methods get children to recognize that these words are spelled differently, while context clues get them to recognize that the words have different meanings.

The main goal of teaching homophones is to help children connect the correct meaning with a particular spelling. We use direct instruction, modeling and demonstrating how to learn homophone pairs. In the process, we can check for understanding and give feedback to children, as well as identify weaknesses in skills in order to plan daily R-T-P lessons.

Struggling readers may need extensive practice, both visual and auditory, with reading the words in context before they can reliably distinguish between homophones.

HOMOPHONES

one, won	break, brake	fare, fair
week, weak	weight, wait	or, oar
meet, meat	they're, there, their	made, maid
rode, road	I, eye	peek, peak
blew, blue	know, no	heel, heal
hour, our	piece, peace	pale, pail
flower, flour	sun, son	tail, tale
pain, pane	knew, new	through, threw
dew, due	hear, here	your, you're
in, inn	see, sea	sail, sale
ring, wring	write, right	herd, heard
not, knot	wood, would	scent, cent, sent
deer, dear	beat, beet	

Picturing Homophones

Materials Laminated "picture cards" with simple illustrations for each homophone pair (see example)

"Picture cards" are a good visual device for connecting meaning to each homophone. Divide a half sheet of tagboard into two sections and write a homophone in each section (*see, sea*). Under each word, sketch or glue a picture showing what it means.

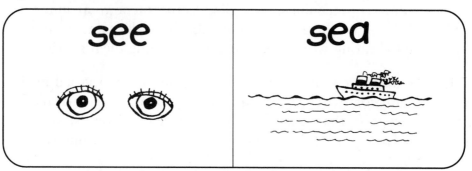

Because some of these words are difficult to picture, you might involve the children in selecting or drawing pictures that suggest the word's meaning to them. Sometimes there may be an elaborate story context for the illustration, and the picture reminds them of that story. Children can read independently through stacks of these cards to practice linking each spelling to its meaning.

Variation: The Other Homophone When children have gained some expertise with meanings and spellings of sets of homophones, you might cut each picture card in half. Present a single homophone card and its picture.

- Children orally read the word.

- They tell you the meaning of the word.

- They then spell and explain the meaning of the other word in the homophone pair.

This activity helps transfer homophones to children's long-term memories.

Mnemonic Aids to Teach Homophones

Materials Laminated index cards, each with one homophone pair that can be linked to a mnemonic aid

Teaching children mnemonic aids is one good way to help them discriminate between homophones. Each mnemonic aid helps children remember the spelling of one word in a homophone pair. Once they know the spelling of one of the words, they can figure out the other one by the process of elimination.

- Show a card with a homophone pair, such as *hear* and *here*.

- Tell children how they can remember the way to spell *hear*: "The word *ear* is inside the word *hear*, and you *hear* with your *ear*."

- Draw a box around the letters *ear*.

- Children then orally explain the meaning of the other homophone in the pair, *here*.

Teach each pair in this way, adding simple drawings or boxing letters wherever possible to reinforce the word meaning.

Following are examples of mnemonic aids that many struggling readers have found useful. Be aware that mnemonics are idiosyncratic—what works for one person won't necessarily work for everyone. Encourage children to make up personal mnemonics that work for them.

Mnemonic Aids to Teach Homophones

1. sea, see — The two *e*'s look like two eyes; you *see* with your eyes.

2. here, hear — The word *ear* is inside the word *hear*; you hear with your ear.

3. meet, meat — The word *eat* is inside the word *meat*; you eat meat.

4. peak, peek — The two *e*'s look like two eyes; eyes can *peek*.

5. weak, week — The two *e*'s are a pair like Saturday and Sunday; Saturday and Sunday are days of the *week*.

6. road, rode — *Rode* is the past tense of *ride*; *ride* and *rode* have the same jump-over spelling pattern.

7. heal, heel — The two *e*'s are like two feet; your *heels* are on your feet.

8. in, inn — The spelling *i-n-n* is found in Holiday *Inn* and Days *Inn*; these are hotels, and *inns* are hotels.

9. or, oar — The two vowels in *oar* are like two paddles on a boat; an *oar* is a paddle.

10. I, eye   The two *e*'s stand for two eyes; you see with your eyes.

11. sail, sale   Seeing a "for sale" sign means something is on sale; if it's for sale you can buy it.

12. know, no   N-o spells *no.*

13. herd, heard   The word *ear* is inside the word *heard;* you heard it with your ear.

14. peace, piece   The word *pie* is inside the word *piece;* you would like a piece of pie to eat.

15. sent, cent   The *c* in *cent* can be turned into a cent sign; a cent sign means money.

16. your, you're   *You're* means *you are;* use *you are* in place of *you're* in a sentence.

17. there, they're   *They're* means *they are;* use *they are* in place of *they're* in a sentence.

18. there, their   The vowels *e* and *i* together are like husband and wife; they live together in *their* house.

Reading Homophones in Sentences

Materials   Laminated sentence strips with fill-in-the-blank homophone choices (see suggested sentences, p. 79); water-based markers

Children should have had direct instruction in all the homophone pairs, either with "picture cards" or mnemonic aids, before you present these sentences. Reading the words in context and choosing the correct spelling reinforces what they have already learned.

- Children orally read each sentence and think about the context clues, picturing the meaning in their minds.

- They match their mental picture to the correct homophone under the blank, circle it, and write it on the blank line.

- For additional practice, ask children to illustrate or tell the meaning of the other homophone in the pair.

Readers who are having trouble with these sentences need more work with picturing homophones or developing their own mnemonic aids.

Sentences with Homophones

1. After lunch, _____ you please wash the dishes for me?
   (wood, would)

2. The strong wind _____ my hat off my head.
   (blew, blue)

3. That is _____ house because we paid for it.
   (hour, our)

4. There are seven days in a _____.
   (week, weak)

5. Mom got out the _____ to bake a pie.
   (flower, flour)

6. Put some salt and pepper on your _____.
   (meet, meat)

7. That _____ in the vase smells nice. I like its _____.
   (flour, flower)   (sent, scent)

8. I can't _____ the TV. There is too much noise in _____.
   (here, hear)   (here, hear)

9. The desk and chair are both made of _____.
   (would, wood)

10. When you can tell time, you know what the _____ is.
    (hour, our)

11. Our _____ car shines because it is so clean.
    (knew, new)

12. We drive on the _____ side of the _____.
                   (write, right)   (road, rode)

13. When my _____ was born, he was very small.
               (sun, son)

14. When we go to the beach, we can swim in the _____.
                                                 (sea, see)

15. I can pay for the gum because it costs just one _____.
                                             (scent, cent)

16. We walked _____ the store and looked for the cheese.
              (through, threw)

17. If I am late, please _____ for me.
                 (weight, wait)

18. My dog always wags his _____ when I come home.
                  (tail, tale)

◆ DAILY R-T-P ◆

Use daily oral practice for homophone pairs that are still difficult for the children. Call out the meanings for a particular pair: "a male child (*son*); it shines in the sky (*sun*)." Children listen to your clues and orally spell the homophone that matches each clue.

SYNONYMS AND ANTONYMS

VOCABULARY SKILL 3: Identify words that have similar meanings (synonyms) and opposite meanings (antonyms).

Synonyms are words that have the same or similar meanings; antonyms are words that have opposite or almost opposite meanings. Children need to learn synonyms and antonyms to develop a reserve of words that will improve their reading comprehension.

As children increase their vocabularies, their fluency and comprehension increase. We expect children to use their phonics skills to read these words, but they will also need context clues to visualize and understand what they read. Although we group synonyms and antonyms under the same skill, we generally teach them separately, synonyms first.

If children mix up the terms *synonym* and *antonym,* point out that *synonym* and *same* begin with the same letter. This mnemonic aid helps them remember synonyms are words that have the same meaning.

Some synonyms have very close to the same meaning and are used interchangeably. It's hard, for example, to explain the difference between *small* and *little,* or *big* and *large.* For words like these, children need only recognize the words as synonyms.

Other synonyms have different shades of meaning that distinguish them. *Big,* for example, describes something that is larger than normal. *Gigantic* is a synonym for *big,* but more precisely, it describes something much larger than big, something fit for a giant. A similar distinction can be made between *little* and *tiny.* Readers who understand the subtle differences between synonyms paint a better mental picture as they read.

When we teach synonyms, we need to help children explore and understand whether or not two words that "mean the same" have different connotations or more precise meanings. This is best done through direct instruction.

As children play the synonym matching game and make word webs as described in the next two activities, talk with them about any subtle differences among word meanings.

- If the synonyms are adjectives, such as *big, large, huge, enormous, great,* and *vast,* talk about the different sorts of things each might be used to describe.

- If the synonyms are verbs, such as *jump, hop, leap, skip, spring,* and *vault,* talk about the different circumstances in which each would most likely be used.

Role-playing is another way to get at the distinctions. Ask children to demonstrate the difference between *laugh, giggle, chuckle, snicker, guffaw,* and *smirk.*

SYNONYM PAIRS

jump, hop	road, street	shout, yell
little, small	big, large	hurry, rush
boat, ship	begin, start	push, shove
quick, fast	high, tall	cent, penny
enjoy, like	woods, forest	noise, sound
race, run	shop, store	name, title
kind, nice	build, make	sick, ill
happy, glad	story, tale	correct, right
ocean, sea	tell, say	night, evening
easy, simple	sleep, doze	strange, odd

Synonym Matching Game

Materials   Sets of synonym cards, including at least 30 synonym pairs, one word per card (prepare from list above)

In this card game, the object is to make three "books" of synonyms to win the game.

- Deal six cards to each player.

- Place the remaining cards facedown in a draw pile. Turn the top card of the draw pile faceup and place it alongside to form the discard pile.

- The player to the left of the dealer goes first. In turn, players look at their cards for any matches they may have to make a book.

- Players who have a book place the two cards together faceup on the table, read the words orally to the group, and explain what they mean, including any slight differences between them.

- The player may then draw the top card from either the draw pile or the discard pile.

- If the card drawn makes a book with a card in their hand, they place the cards on the table and read them orally to the group. If the drawn card does not match, it is placed faceup in the discard pile.

Play continues clockwise. The first player to make three books of synonyms wins the game.

THREE "BOOKS" OF SYNONYMS

jump hop   little small   boat ship

Variation: More Synonyms As children gain knowledge of synonyms, add additional cards to the deck so each "book" is three or four synonyms instead of a pair.

Synonym Word Webs

Materials   Reference list of synonym web-starter words below

For making word webs, children draw on their prior knowledge to connect words that have almost the same meaning. When the activity is done in a group, the children learn from one another. Using a familiar word like *big,* children orally brainstorm other words with the same or similar meanings. Write their ideas on a large word web for visual display and discussion.

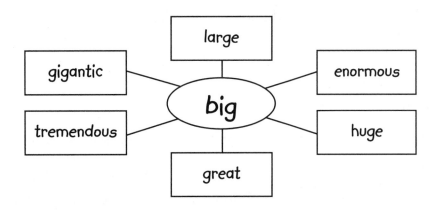

SYNONYM WEB-STARTER WORDS

happy	little	road	jump	make
sad	big	boat	walk	laugh
fast	tall	house	run	shout
easy	short	dirt	fly	look
hard	thin	money	like	say

Variation: Synonym Mobiles Display the word webs on simple mobiles. As children learn new synonyms, they can add these to the appropriate mobiles.

Choosing Synonyms in Sentences

Materials   Pairs of laminated sentence strips (see suggested sentences below); water-based markers

When children encounter synonyms in sentence context, they can recognize more easily that in a synonym pair, the words may have slightly different meanings. Present pairs of sentences for children to read orally. Using context clues, they choose the better synonym for each sentence. For example:

- The chocolate chip cookie is (large, enormous), so I can share it with my friend.

- The wedding cake is (large, enormous), and it will serve 200 people.

Large and *enormous* mean almost the same thing, but *enormous* describes something that is bigger than *large*. Children visualize a large cookie and focus on the context clue *share it with my friend*. They also visualize a wedding cake and focus on the context clue *it will serve 200 people*. From this information, they circle and read the better synonym for each sentence.

Sentence Pairs with Synonyms

1. The (ship, boat) floated across the small lake in the park.

   The (ship, boat) carried a load of oil across the ocean.

2. I saw a little frog (hop, jump) across the grass.

   The boy had to (hop, jump) high to reach the tree branch.

3. A flea is a (small, tiny) bug that is hard to see on dogs.

   A ladybug is a (small, tiny) bug that you might see on a leaf.

4. Those pants are too (tremendous, large) for me, so I can't wear them.

   The elephant looked (tremendous, large) next to the small white puppy.

5. They will (race, run) down the hill to see who gets there first.

   They (race, run) around on the grass when they play tag.

6. The (name, title) of that book is *Where the Wild Things Are*.

   The (name, title) of that street is Main Street.

7. Mother gave us a small (snack, meal) of cookies and milk after school.

   Mother cooked hot dogs and french fries for our evening (snack, meal).

8. The buildings in the city are (high, tall).

   The jet plane flew (high, tall) above the city.

Antonym Matching Game

Materials   Sets of antonym cards, including at least 30 antonym pairs, one word per card (prepare from list, p. 86)

In this card game, the object is to make three "books" of antonyms to win the game.

- Deal six cards to each player.

- Place the remaining cards facedown in a draw pile. Turn the top card of the draw pile faceup and place it alongside to form the discard pile.

- The player to the left of the dealer goes first. In turn, players look at their cards for any matches they may have to make a book.

- Players who can make a book place the two cards together faceup on the table, read the words to the group, and tell what they mean.

- The player may then draw the top card from either the draw pile or the discard pile.

- If the card drawn makes a book with a card in their hand, they place the cards on the table and read them to the group.

- If the drawn card does not match, it is placed faceup in the discard pile.

- Play continues clockwise. The first player to make three books of antonyms wins the game.

THREE "BOOKS" OF ANTONYMS

up   down   all   none   new   old

ANTONYM PAIRS

up–down	all–none	old–new
lost–found	over–under	old–young
wet–dry	off–on	short–tall
hot–cold	slow–fast	give–take
in–out	night–day	good–bad
bottom–top	first–last	early–late
open–shut	spend–save	lost–found
buy–sell	big–little	weak–strong
fancy–plain	quiet–noisy	rough–smooth
north–south	happy–sad	sharp–dull

Choosing Antonyms in Sentences

Materials   Laminated sentence strips (see suggested sentences below); water-based markers

When children read sentences in which they must choose the correct antonym from a pair, they must use context clues to picture the intended meaning. Present sentences for children to read orally. They choose and circle the antonym that best fits the sentence and orally reread to make sure the sentence makes sense.

Sentences with Antonyms

1. My mother cooked us a (cold, hot) meal last night.

2. The (weak, strong) ox pulled the heavy cart with ease.

3. We woke up (late, early), so we did not get to school on time.

4. The (old, young) puppy is very playful and runs around a lot.

5. The ice under our skates was as (rough, smooth) as silk.

6. You need a (sharp, dull) knife to slice this bread because the crust is very hard.

7. It was very cold last night, so we slept (under, over) three quilts.

8. I need it to be (noisy, quiet) when I read my book.

9. I am trying to (save, spend) my money so I will have lots for our trip.

10. The line leader is the (last, first) one in line.

"Word walls" with lists of synonyms and antonyms can be used daily for a quick review and practice session. Children can orally read the lists or write their own sentences using words from the lists.

MULTIPLE-MEANING WORDS

VOCABULARY SKILL 4: Recognize in context the appropriate meaning for a multiple-meaning word.

Many words in our language have more than one meaning. When struggling learners encounter such a word in their reading, they need to be aware of the multiple meanings, and they need to be able to select the meaning that works for that particular sentence.

Context clues help with this task, but children must also draw on their prior knowledge of such words. When we teach multiple-meaning words in oral activities, presenting the words in a clear context, children expand the reserve of words they take into their reading experiences.

If you look up the word *run* in the dictionary, you may find more than thirty meanings listed. Children will know some of these and not know others. Our goal is to increase their knowledge, day by day, so they are better equipped to make good decisions about multiple-meaning words they find in their reading. Here is a short sample of the meanings of *run*:

1. (verb) to go quickly by moving the legs more rapidly than by walking

2. (verb) to make a quick trip for a short stay somewhere

3. (verb) to flow or rush, as water

4. (noun) a long hole in knit fabric where stitches have come undone

5. (noun) a point scored in baseball by touching all the bases in order

When children read, "The boys *run* all the way to school," they will likely visualize boys running down the street because they have prior knowledge of definition 1. When they read, "Mom is going to *run* to the store to buy some milk," they will probably visualize someone making a quick trip to the store, in a car rather than on foot, because they have prior knowledge of definition 2.

But when children read, "The stream *runs* through a grove of pine trees," they may not accurately visualize what that means if they have no prior knowledge of definition 3. Similarly, when they read, "Oh no! I have a big *run* in my tights," they will be unable to visualize what is happening if they have no prior knowledge of definition 4. When they read, "The Braves won the game by two *runs*," many will know exactly what this means because they have prior knowledge of definition 5.

From an experience like this, we know that we must teach definitions 3 and 4, perhaps by showing a picture, by role-playing, and by talking about the definitions. Active discussion of the words, with visual aids and role playing, is more effective for struggling learners than asking them to memorize a list of definitions.

Reading Multiple-Meaning Words in Phrases

Materials   Resource list of multiple-meaning words in phrases (p. 89)

Even when children already know the various meanings of a multiple-meaning word, they need to focus on context clues and picture the situation in their minds in order to know which meaning is intended. Use this oral and kinesthetic technique, writing phrases on the board or on chart paper, for practice with multiple-meaning words.

- Start by writing the phrase *bark like a dog.* Underline the word *bark.*
- Children respond by barking like a dog.
- Next, write the phrase *the rough bark on the tree trunk* and underline the word *bark.*
- Children can respond with pantomime, as if they are feeling the bark of a tree with their fingers.
- Continue the activity with the other pairs of phrases.

Alternatively, children might illustrate the two phrases. In either case, they must actively think about the underlined word and use context clues to understand the definition intended.

Phrases with Multiple-Meaning Words

wave good-bye	*fall* down
wave in the ocean	the season is *fall*
put it in the *box*	the plane will *land*
draw a *box*	the *land* is flat
saw the wood	the *ring* is shiny
we *saw* you	*ring* the bell
the bird's *bill* is sharp	hit the ball with the *bat*
pay the telephone *bill*	the *bat* flew around the streetlight
the fish has *scales*	Cinderella went to the *ball*
scales can weigh you	hit the *ball*
write your name with a *pen*	the river has a wide *mouth*
herd the sheep into their *pen*	close your *mouth*
pour the milk from the *pitcher*	*cross* the street
the *pitcher* throws the ball	*cross* the letter *t*
tip of your finger	wash your hands in the *sink*
tip over the trash can	a ship can *sink*
the river *bank*	it is not *fair*
get money from the *bank*	she has blonde hair and *fair* skin

Reading Multiple-Meaning Words in Sentences

Materials   Laminated list of sentence pairs (prepare from list, p. 90); water-based markers. If children are still struggling with print, present these on laminated sentence strips.

After oral work interpreting multiple-meaning words in phrases, children can practice what they have learned by matching definitions to multiple-meaning words in sentences. They orally read each pair of sentences and the two definitions that follow. Then they write the letter of the matching definition (*a* or *b*) in the blank after each sentence.

Sentence Pairs with Multiple-Meaning Words

1. A rock will <u>sink</u> to the bottom of the river. _____

   Wash your hands with soap and water in the <u>sink</u>. _____

       a. place to wash

       b. fall through water

2. The gas <u>bill</u> was very large this month. _____

   The bird's <u>bill</u> was pointy and sharp. _____

       a. beak

       b. money you owe

3. The <u>bat</u> flew around in the cave. _____

   Tom uses a wooden <u>bat</u> to play baseball. _____

       a. stick used to hit a ball

       b. animal that flies at night

4. I got on the <u>scales</u> to find out my weight. _____

   The snake's <u>scales</u> felt smooth to the touch. _____

       a. thin, flat plates on the skin of some animals

       b. device for weighing

5. The queen danced with the king all night at the <u>ball</u>. _____

   Grandpa tossed the <u>ball</u> to the little boy in the backyard. _____

       a. toy that you can throw, bounce, and catch

       b. fancy dance

6. I <u>saw</u> you playing at the park yesterday. _____

   Dad will <u>saw</u> the wood in two pieces. _____

       a. cut with a sharp tool

       b. looked at

7. The phone will <u>ring</u> when someone calls you. _____

   Nan's shiny gold <u>ring</u> fell off her finger. _____

       a. make a bell sound

       b. circle of metal

8. My mother always uses a black <u>pen</u> when she writes. _____

   The pigs live in a muddy <u>pen</u> next to the barn. _____

    a. small, closed yard for animals

    b. writing tool

Defining Multiple-Meaning Words in Sentences

Materials   Laminated list of sentences (prepare from list below); water-based markers. If children are still struggling with print, present these on laminated sentence strips.

When children are reading, they will usually not encounter multiple-meaning words in pairs. Instead, they will read one such word in a sentence and have to decide which meaning fits. This technique offers practice with that skill.

- Present a sentence with a multiple-meaning word and three possible definitions.

- Children orally read the sentence and the definitions.

- They think about what the context clues mean, picture the sentence in their mind, and circle the correct definition.

- Encourage children to ask themselves about their final choice, "Does that make sense?"

Since this is more difficult than previous activities, it should be used after children have had considerable practice with multiple-meaning words.

Sentences with Multiple-Meaning Words

1. Mom and Dad sat on the <u>bank</u> of the river so they could watch the children fish.

   a. place to keep money
   b. tilt airplane wings
   c. the land next to water

2. My baseball team <u>beat</u> the other team last week.

   a. stirred quickly
   b. got a higher score
   c. hit with a stick

3. My dad's boss will not <u>fire</u> him if he always does good work.

    a. make someone leave his job
    b. throw with great force
    c. something burning

4. We set the flag into a <u>stand</u> because it is too heavy for someone to hold.

    a. booth where things are sold
    b. be up on two feet
    c. holder

5. Please get the wooden <u>ruler</u> so I can draw a six-inch line.

    a. king or queen
    b. boss
    c. measuring tool

6. The sailors knew they would be home soon when they saw <u>land</u> from their ship.

    a. come down after jumping
    b. bring an airplane down
    c. solid ground

7. The <u>point</u> of my father's talk was to teach me to follow all the rules.

    a. place where two lines meet
    b. sharp edge or tip
    c. purpose or reason

8. The policeman saw a <u>figure</u> of a man running out of the bank.

    a. shape or form
    b. number
    c. picture or diagram

9. Most of the sheep were in the field, but the <u>rams</u> were kept in a pen.

    a. football team
    b. bumps into
    c. male sheep

10. For my vacation, I will <u>fly</u> to California and go to the San Diego Zoo.

    a. baseball hit high in the air
    b. travel through the air
    c. winged insect

Quick, daily reviews of multiple-meaning words help struggling learners develop their vocabulary and read with increased comprehension. There are many multiple-meaning words in addition to those included in the activities in this chapter; a few are listed below. Keep a growing collection of these for daily practice. Encourage children to bring in further examples for a word wall.

Additional Multiple-Meaning Words

change your clothes
pocket full of *change*

star in the night sky
movie *star*

computer *bug*
garden *bug*

light from a lamp
light meaning not heavy

ground meat
fall on the *ground*

stamp your feet
stamp on a letter

warm winter *coat*
coat of paint

flower *bed*
bed you sleep in

trip and fall
go on a *trip*

leaves on a tree
leaves the scene

snakes *shed* their skin
garden *shed*

sign your name
sign on a store window

mail a *letter*
letter of the alphabet

park your car
play in the *park*

honk your car *horn*
horn of a bull

train your dog
catch a *train*

bike *tires*
tires as in gets tired

lamp *shade*
shade of a tree

COMPOUND WORDS

STRUCTURAL SKILL 1: Recognize the parts of a compound word and the meaning of the whole word.

Compound words are two words joined together to make a new word. The resulting longer words are sometimes overwhelming for struggling learners. By the same token, finding that they can read compound words gives children an immediate feeling of success and helps them overcome their fear of words with many letters.

We teach children that compound words are made up of little words joined together, and by using their phonics skills to read each little word, they can easily read the big word. Teaching them to analyze compound words in this way reduces the frequency of guessing or just skipping those words.

When children have difficulty understanding the meaning of a compound word, they usually have limited prior knowledge of one or both of the two smaller words. For example, understanding the word *snowplow* can be difficult if children don't know what a plow is. This confusion can be overcome by discussing the meaning of smaller word, and then the meaning of the whole.

Reading Compound Words

Materials | Laminated cards for compound words (prepare from list, p. 95); highlighters in two colors

With this visual technique, children take compound words apart, orally read each smaller word, and then read them together as one word. Children use highlighters to mark each smaller word with a different color. This makes each little word stand out so visual learners can more easily see them within the longer one.

Many compounds are concrete nouns that are easy for young readers to visualize in their minds. Less picturable are the many compounds that begin with *some, any,* and *every.* However, it's important that children learn to read and spell these more abstract compounds because they appear with high frequency in standard reading materials.

COMPOUND WORDS

airplane	driveway	mailbox	seafood
airport	fireplace	maybe	seashell
baseball	firewood	moonlight	seaweed
basketball	fireworks	myself	snowball
bathtub	flashlight	oatmeal	snowflake
beanbag	football	paintbrush	snowplow
bedtime	footprint	pancake	starfish
beehive	goalpost	peanut	sunlight
bulldog	goldfish	railroad	sunset
classmate	headlight	rainbow	teapot
cupcake	heartbeat	raincoat	treetop
daydream	hillside	sailboat	weekend

anyone	someone	everyone
anything	something	everything
anywhere	somewhere	everywhere
anytime	someday	everyday
anyway	sometime	

Reading Compound Words in Sentences

Materials   Laminated sentence strips (see suggested sentences, pp. 95–96); water-based markers

When we present compound words in sentences, children use context clues to make sense of the words. With this technique:

- Children orally read a fill-in-the-blank sentence with a given choice of two similar-looking compound words.

- Using context clues, they visualize what is happening and think about which compound word best fits the sentence.

- They circle their choice and write it in the blank.

Sentences with Compound Words

1. Our little dog can play in our _____ because it has a fence.
   (backbone, backyard)

2. The large jets circle around the _____ until they can land.
   (airport, airplane)

3. My sister plays first base for her _____ team.
   (ballpark, softball)

4. The bright _____ hurt my eyes, so I put on my sunglasses.
   (sunlight, sunset)

5. Mom told me I could go _____ I wanted on my birthday.
   (anywhere, anything)

6. The _____ made the roads white with snow.
   (thunderstorm, snowstorm)

7. My dad stacked the _____ in a tall pile in the backyard.
   (fireplace, firewood)

8. Tom loves to eat fish, clams, and other kinds of _____.
   (seafood, seaweed)

9. During the strong windstorm, dry leaves blew _____.
   (everyone, everywhere)

10. I put on my _____ to walk home in the rain.
    (rainbow, raincoat)

• DAILY R-T-P •

Quick, daily reviews of compound words help struggling learners develop their vocabulary and read with increased comprehension. There are many compound words in addition to those included in the activities in this chapter. Keep a growing collection of these for daily oral practice. Encourage children to bring in further examples for a word wall.

CONTRACTIONS

STRUCTURAL SKILL 2: Recognize contractions as a short form of two other words.

When we speak, we often run two words together as one word and leave out some sounds, usually from the second word. Instead of *he would,* for example, we often say *he'd;* instead of *she is,* we often say *she's.* Contractions are the way we show this in writing. In a contraction, we write two words together, putting an apostrophe in place of the missing letters.

Children need to understand that contractions began as two words, and that a contraction means the same thing that the original two words did. Because the contraction and the two words are interchangeable, children should be able to substitute one for the other.

Thus, we teach children to read, spell, and understand common pairs of words and change them into a contraction. Ultimately children should be able to reverse this process, changing a contraction back to the original two words.

Struggling readers can have trouble making this link and will sometimes substitute an incorrect contraction for the two original words. For example, children often substitute *doesn't* for *do not.* To help prevent this, we tell children that the spelling of the first word usually stays the same and only the spelling of the second word is changed.

Another way we help them is by teaching contractions in groups, so they see the consistent spelling patterns for contractions made with *is, are, will, have, not,* and *would.*

Making Contractions

Materials   Laminated lists of words that make common contractions (prepare from lists, p. 98); water-based markers

For a kinesthetic and visual technique to help children read and spell common contractions, prepare lists of two-word combinations. Make six separate lists for contractions of *is, are, will, not, have,* and *would.* Include a writing blank after each word pair.

On a seventh list, include *I am* (*I'm*) and *let us* (*let's*), which are unique, plus these variations on the *not* pattern: *cannot* (one word changes to *can't*), *do not* (follows the spelling pattern, but the pronunciation changes), and *will not* (changes to *won't,* which rhymes with *don't*). Teach these exceptions separately.

CONTRACTION LISTS

Contractions with *is*

he is	he's
she is	she's
it is	it's
here is	here's
that is	that's
there is	there's
how is	how's
who is	who's
where is	where's

Contractions with *are*

you are	you're
we are	we're
they are	they're

Contractions with *will*

I will	I'll
you will	you'll
he will	he'll
she will	she'll
we will	we'll
they will	they'll
that will	that'll

Contractions with *have*

I have	I've
you have	you've
we have	we've
they have	they've

Contractions with *not*

is not	isn't
are not	aren't
has not	hasn't
have not	haven't
had not	hadn't
was not	wasn't
were not	weren't
does not	doesn't
did not	didn't
would not	wouldn't
could not	couldn't
should not	shouldn't

Contractions with *would*

I would	I'd
you would	you'd
he would	he'd
she would	she'd
we would	we'd
they would	they'd

Some exceptions

I am	I'm
let us	let's
cannot	can't
do not	don't
will not	won't

For each list:

- Children read the two words on the left side of the list.

- They use water-based markers to highlight the letters in the second word that will be replaced by an apostrophe.

- They then write and spell the corresponding contraction in the blank.

Variation: Identifying the Two Words Reverse the process, supplying a list of contractions. Children change each contraction back into the original two words.

Build a Contraction

Materials Build-a-Contraction board (prepare on half-sheet of poster board, as illustrated); sets of two-word cards and contraction cards (prepare from lists, p. 98)

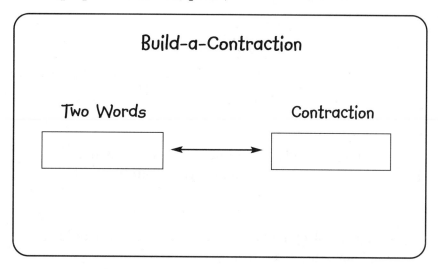

Set up the Build-a-Contraction board and place contraction cards facedown in a pile near the board.

• Deal out two-word cards evenly to the players.

• Children take turns drawing one card from the contraction pile and trying to match it to one of the two-word cards they are holding.

• If they find a match, they place both cards on the board under the correct headings.

• If they cannot make a match, they place the contraction card at the bottom of the contraction pile.

• Play continues until one player has no more two-word cards left; that player wins the game.

Variation: Reverse Match Play the same game but reverse the cards. That is, deal out contraction cards to the players, and place the two-word cards facedown in a pile.

Reading Contractions in Sentences

Materials Laminated sentence strips (see suggested sentences below); water-based markers or highlighters

Children orally read each sentence. They then circle the correct substitution for the underlined word or words and read the sentence again, substituting the word or words they have circled. This technique helps children understand the meaning of contractions as they see that two words and their contraction can be used interchangeably in the same sentence.

Sentences with Contractions

1. There's a cat stuck up in the tree. <u>I would</u> like you to get it down.
   (I'll, I'd)

2. I'd like to jump rope but <u>you'd</u> rather skate.
   (you are, you would)

3. <u>They'd</u> sleep late every day if their mom would let them.
   (They will, They would)

4. We were on a field trip this morning, so we <u>were not</u> in class.
   (we're, weren't)

5. Jack <u>doesn't</u> want to wear a shirt with green and blue stripes.
   (do not, does not)

6. That glass of juice <u>isn't</u> yours. It is mine.
   (it is, is not)

7. Jan <u>hasn't</u> been to any of my ball games. I hope she comes today.
   (has not, how is)

8. Some of that milk in the jug is for us. <u>Do not</u> use it all.
   (Doesn't, Don't)

9. I <u>will not</u> carry all those books by myself. Please help me.
   (won't, want)

10. Where did we park the car? We <u>cannot</u> find it anywhere.
    (we're, can't)

11. Can you help me find my skates? <u>I've</u> left them somewhere.
    (I have, I will)

12. You like to read. Tell me which books <u>you have</u> read.
    (you've, you're)

13. Don't you love the zoo? <u>I'm</u> glad you could come with me.
    (I will, I am)

14. If my dad says I can have a pet, <u>I'll</u> get a dog.
    (I am, I will)

15. If you cannot find your ball, <u>we'll</u> help you look for it.
    (we are, we will)

16. Check your watch to find out if <u>you are</u> late.
    (you've, you're)

17. The Cubs haven't lost a game. <u>They are</u> the best baseball team in town.
    (They'll, They're)

18. <u>Where's</u> your mom now? I need to talk to her.
    (Where is, We are)

Contractions can be difficult for some children because there are so many of them. Continue to check for understanding through daily practice, then teach or reteach according to the needs of your struggling learners.

The Reading Tools chart (p. 49) is useful for review of contractions and their spelling patterns. In the box headed Contractions, the marked-out letters indicate the spelling pattern for that set of contractions. Present word pairs, such as *who is, they are, you have,* and so forth, asking children to show which pattern they would follow to make a contraction in each case.

SPELLING CHANGES WITH COMMON SUFFIXES

STRUCTURAL SKILL 3: Recognize the root words, suffixes, and spelling changes involved in making plurals, verb forms, and comparative forms.

Plural endings *-s* and *-es* (*cats, brushes*), verb endings *-ing* and *-ed* (*going, looked*), and comparative endings *-er* and *-est* (*faster, coldest*) are a natural part of children's oral vocabularies. When struggling readers can identify these endings in print, they can then focus more easily on the root word (also called *base* word), which they then decode by using the phonics principles and spelling patterns they already know.

Adding these common endings sometimes involves a spelling change in the root word. We may double the final consonant (*tugged, fatter*); we may drop the silent *e* (*saving, hoping*); or we may change the final *y* to an *i* (*carried, happier*). These spelling changes can make it difficult, particularly for visual learners, to identify and decode the root word.

Through word-building activities, children learn to analyze these spelling changes, a process they can then reverse to dissect and recognize words they encounter in their reading.

Reading Plural Endings -s and -es

Materials   Laminated list of singular words (prepare from list, p. 103); water-based markers or highlighters

Through this visual and kinesthetic technique, children choose which plural suffix (*-s* or *-es*) to add to a singular root word. We teach them to focus on the specific letter or letters at the end of the word.

Write on the board the letters *x, z, ss, ch,* and *sh.* Explain that if the root word ends in one of those letters or digraphs, we must add *-es* to make the word plural. Present an example for each one, such as *box/boxes, waltz/waltzes, loss/losses, watch/watches, bush/bushes.* With most other letters at the end of the singular root word, children will simply add *-s* to make the word plural.

After this introduction, proceed as follows:

- Present a laminated list of singular words.

- Children circle or highlight any ending letters that require them to add *-es.*

- After each word on the list, children write its plural form.

ROOT WORDS AND THEIR PLURAL FORMS

dish	dishes	pillow	pillows
peach	peaches	letter	letters
box	boxes	rabbit	rabbits
brush	brushes	dress	dresses
cap	caps	watch	watches
dog	dogs	guess	guesses
star	stars	fox	foxes
mitten	mittens	bunch	bunches
chick	chicks	wish	wishes
seal	seals	tax	taxes
book	books	waltz	waltzes
block	blocks	ash	ashes
glass	glasses	patch	patches
wax	waxes	class	classes

Distinguishing Singular and Plural Forms in Sentences

Materials   Laminated sentence strips (see suggested sentences, p. 104); water-based markers

Children read each sentence orally, think about context clues, decide whether the singular or plural form best fits the sentence, and circle the correct word to complete the sentence. For example, "My mom and dad need two (*dish, dishes*) to eat their lunch." The words *mom and dad* and *two* are context clues that indicate the word *dish* should be plural. By picturing the meaning of the sentence, children understand that *dishes* is the correct answer.

Sentences with Singular and Plural Words

1. When I look up in the sky, I see many _____ shining.
   (star, stars)

2. Only one player on my baseball team wore a red _____.
   (cap, caps)

3. On cold days I wear my _____ to keep my hands warm.
   (mitten, mittens)

4. When we moved, we had many _____ to pack.
   (box, boxes)

5. We had six _____ to wash after we ate our lunch.
   (glass, glasses)

6. The man at the zoo threw fish to feed the seven _____ .
   (seal, seals)

7. Sue needs a _____ to brush her dog.
   (brush, brushes)

8. Mom packed one sweet _____ in my lunch box.
   (peach, peaches)

9. Wolves and _____ look a lot like dogs.
   (fox, foxes)

10. Dad gave me a _____ on my cheek as I left for school.
    (kiss, kisses)

Word Building with Spelling Changes

Materials Spelling Changes board (prepare on poster board, with a title and four equal columns, as illustrated); set of laminated word-building cards (prepare from list, p. 108); water-based markers

Spelling Changes			
Double Final Consonant	Drop Silent e	Change y → i	No Change

This kinesthetic and visual word-building technique features a two-step process to help children identify root words for which adding a suffix changes the spelling of the root word.

- In the first step, children look at a root word and determine what pattern it follows, according to the Spelling Changes board.

- In the second step, children change the spelling of the root word and add the suffix.

Make a set of laminated word-building cards by writing a root word, a plus sign, and a suffix on each card. Underneath, draw a line where children can write the new word, which may or may not show a spelling change. Include words for each category on the Spelling Changes board.

SAMPLE WORD-BUILDING CARDS

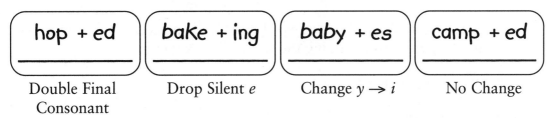

hop + ed	bake + ing	baby + es	camp + ed
Double Final Consonant	Drop Silent e	Change y → i	No Change

Give specific examples, using word-building cards and the Spelling Changes board, to teach children the three types of spelling changes and words that do not change.

Double Final Consonant When the root word has one vowel and one final consonant, we double the consonant before adding the suffix. For example:

tug + ed → tugged

hop + ing → hopping

sad + er → sadder

Demonstrate with the card for *hop + ed*. Point out one vowel and one final consonant in the root word, underline the consonant that will be doubled, write the new word *hopped* on the line, and then place the card on the board under the heading "Double Final Consonant."

Drop Silent *e* When the root word ends in a silent *e*, we drop the *e* before adding the suffix. For example:

hope + ing → hoping

bake + ed → baked

fine + er → finer

This pattern can be confusing when the suffix itself starts with an *e*, because it appears that the spelling of the root word has *not* changed. You can point out that we drop the *e* so we don't end up with two *e*'s together: *hope + ed → hoped*, not *hopeed*.

Demonstrate the pattern with the card for *bake + ing*. Point out the silent *e*, draw a line through it to indicate that it will be dropped, write the new word *baking* on the line, and then place the card on the board under the heading "Drop Silent *e*."

Change *y* to *i* When the root word ends in a *y* preceded by a consonant, we change the *y* to *i* before adding the suffix. For example:

bunny + es → bunnies

dry + ed → dried

funny + er → funnier

Note that this pattern does *not* hold for adding the suffix *-ing*, because that would result in a repeated letter *i*: *dry + ing → drying*, not *driing*.

Demonstrate this pattern with the card *baby + es*. Point out that the root word *baby* ends in a *y* preceded by a consonant. Circle the *y*, indicating that it will change to an *i* when the suffix is added. Write the new word *babies* on the line and place the card on the board under the heading "Change *y* → *i*."

No Spelling Change For words that do not fall into one of these three patterns, there is generally no spelling change when the suffix is added. For example:

watch + es → watches

melt + ed → melted

sweet + er → sweeter

Demonstrate with the card *camp + ed*. Point out that the root word *camp* has one vowel and two consonants at the end; it does *not* have one vowel and one consonant, or a final silent *e*, or a consonant followed by *y*. Thus there is no spelling change. Write the new word *camped* on the line and place the card under the heading "No Change."

With this technique, children follow the patterns to write words with suffixes and then sort the words into the four columns of the Spelling Changes board.

- Place the word-building cards facedown in a pile.
- Children take turns drawing a card.
- They look at the root word to determine what type of spelling change will take place.
- They use water-based markers to make any changes in the root word and write the new word on the line.
- Finally, they place the card in the correct section of the board.

WORDS TO USE WITH SPELLING CHANGES BOARD

Word Building	Word Dissecting	Word Building	Word Dissecting
Double final consonant		**Change *y* to *i***	
bat + ing	batting	bunny + es	bunnies
big + er	bigger	cherry + es	cherries
big + est	biggest	cry + es	cries
drip + ing	dripping	daisy + es	daisies
hit + ing	hitting	family + es	families
hop + ing	hopping	funny + er	funnier
quit + ing	quitting	happy + est	happiest
red + er	redder	lazy + er	lazier
rub + ed	rubbed	lucky + er	luckier
run + ing	running	muddy + est	muddiest
shop + er	shopper	party + es	parties
swim + er	swimmer	penny + es	pennies
tag + ed	tagged	pretty + est	prettiest
tap + ed	tapped	puppy + es	puppies
tip + ing	tipping	silly + er	sillier
win + er	winner	story + es	stories
zip + ed	zipped	try + ed	tried

Word Building	Word Dissecting	Word Building	Word Dissecting
Drop silent *e*		**No change**	
bake + ed	baked	camp + ing	camping
cute + est	cutest	clean + er	cleaner
hide + ing	hiding	cold + er	colder
hope + ing	hoping	fast + est	fastest
name + ed	named	jump + ed	jumped
rake + ing	raking	loud + er	louder
ride + ing	riding	neat + est	neatest
safe + er	safer	quick + er	quicker
shine + ing	shining	short + er	shorter
skate + ed	skated	sleep + ing	sleeping
slice + ed	sliced	tall + est	tallest
smile + ing	smiling	think + ing	thinking
taste + ed	tasted	trick + ed	tricked
wave + ing	waving	work + er	worker
write + er	writer	yell + ed	yelled

Word Dissecting with Spelling Changes

Materials   Spelling Changes board (from previous activity); laminated word-dissecting cards (prepare from list, p. 108); water-based markers

In a reversal of the word-building process, children examine and dissect words to find root words and suffixes. This technique uses the same Spelling Changes board with a different set of cards. To make each card, write a word to which a suffix has been added and draw a line below where children can write the root word. Include words that involved a spelling change in adding the suffix and words that did not change.

WORD-DISSECTING CARDS

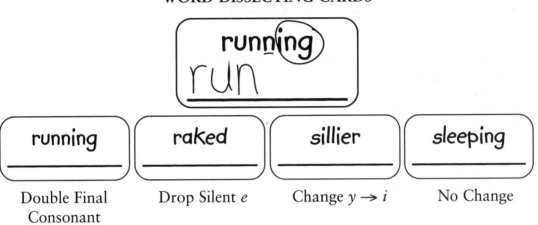

As children take turns drawing a card from the word-dissecting pile, they dissect each word by circling the suffix. They then examine the remaining word part, determine if a spelling change has taken place, and write the root word on the blank line. For example, suppose the card drawn shows the word *running*.

- The children circle the suffix *-ing* with water-based markers and examine the remaining word part, *runn*.

- Children see that the word has an extra *n*, which they underline. This helps them recognize that the spelling change for this word was a doubling of the final consonant.

- They write the root word *run* on the line.

- Finally, they place the card on the board under the heading "Double Final Consonant."

This reverse technique helps children who may have difficulty recognizing root words with suffixes in context because the spelling change makes them look strange. Children build on their experience with word building as they examine and dissect words, using what they know to learn something new.

Placing this structural analysis skill in the hands of the learner greatly increases reading fluency.

Posting a list of common suffixes helps children identify them when using the Spelling Changes board.

Adding Suffixes to Words in Sentences

Materials   Laminated list of fill-in-the-blank sentences (prepare from list below); water-based markers

Children orally read each sentence and think about the context clues. Looking at the root word, they decide which suffix to add so the sentence makes sense. They decide if a spelling change is needed and write the new word in the blank.

Spelling Changes with Common Suffixes

1. I am watching a wild bunny that is _____ across my yard.
(hop)

2. In the summer I like to go _____ in the lake.
(swim)

3. Their dad is _____ them how to build a birdhouse.
(teach)

4. The little baby was _____ at her mother.
(smile)

5. My dog _____ his tail when he saw me coming home.
(wag)

6. The cat _____ the mouse, but it got away.
(chase)

7. On July 4 we _____ hot dogs on the grill.
(roast)

8. The mother bunny had three _____ in her nest.
   (baby)

9. After we picked _____ , my grandmother made a cherry pie.
   (cherry)

10. A nickel is the same as five _____ .
    (penny)

11. There are ten _____ in my class this year.
    (boy)

12. Alex always wins. He is _____ than I am.
    (lucky)

13. My cat sleeps all day and is _____ than my dog.
    (lazy)

14. When Kay scored, she was the _____ girl on the team.
    (happy)

• DAILY R·T·P •

On the Reading Tools chart (second grade teaching tool, p. 49), use the fourth row of boxes to review the spelling changes that can take place when a suffix is added to a root word. Point to each box in turn, asking children to explain what happens to the root word in each case.

- We double the final consonant before adding the suffix because the root word has one vowel and one consonant at the end.
- We drop the silent *e* from the root word before adding the suffix.
- We change the *y* in the root word to an *i* before adding the suffix, because the *y* has a consonant in front of it.

Remind them that the same spelling change will take place even when a different suffix is added to the root word; that is, the word *hop* gets the final *p* doubled whether we are adding *-ing* or *-ed*.

LONG-WORD DECODING

STRUCTURAL SKILL 4: Break long words into smaller parts as an aid to decoding.

When struggling readers encounter a word with many letters, they tend to look at just the beginning letters and guess, sometimes wildly, any word that begins with that sound. They do this because they haven't learned a step-by-step method to attack longer words. With all those letters, the long word doesn't look like any of the spelling patterns children have learned. This frightens them, and fear makes them guess.

To overcome this fear, we teach children a series of simple steps by which they dissect or "chop up" longer words into small parts, use what they know to read each part, and rebuild the words by putting the parts together again.

The first step is for children to box the letters that make one sound, using the phonics skills they have previously learned. In particular, this helps them focus on any initial blends and digraphs and double-vowel or irregular-vowel spelling patterns in the word.

Additionally, if children see the silent *e* "jump-over" pattern, they mark it with an arrow from the *e* to the preceding vowel, just as they did in short words of this pattern. This type of marking is a kinesthetic activity that gets children actively involved with the word.

LETTERS TO BE BOXED

Blends and Digraphs					Double Vowels	Irregular Vowel Patterns	
bl	br	sc	scr	ch	ai	ar	oo
cl	cr	sk	spr	sh	ay	er	ou
fl	dr	sm	str	th	ee	ir	ow
gl	fr	sn	thr	wh	ea	or	oi
pl	gr	sp			ie	ur	oy
sl	pr	st			oe		
	tr	sw			oa		
		tw			ue		

After they have marked the word, children next use a "long-word help card," which shows them a set of codes for dissecting longer words. The codes are a simple way to help the children find syllables in the longer word, each syllable having a vowel sound.

In the codes, C represents a consonant, and V represents a vowel—either a single vowel, or a boxed double-vowel that has a single sound. For example, the CVC code means the first three letters of the long word are consonant, vowel, consonant.

```
┌─────────────────┐
│ LONG-WORD       │
│ HELP CARD       │
│   I. CVC        │
│   2. CCVC       │
│      CVCC       │
│   3. VC         │
└─────────────────┘
```

To use the help card, children look at the first few letters of a longer word to see if they match any of these codes. The numbers 1–3 indicate the order in which they are to try matching the codes to the letters. After they have found a match for the first part of the word, they continue in the same way with the remaining letters.

While children are first learning to use these codes, it usually helps to have them write each matching code under the letters in the word. Most struggling readers will need to do this writing for only a short period of time before they internalize the codes and break longer words apart mentally.

After children box in, label, and break up long words, they are able to use what they know to read the smaller parts. Teaching them to cover the second part of the word while they are reading the first part helps them focus.

Using the Help Card for Long-Word Decoding

Materials   Long-word help card for each student (prepare on index cards, as illustrated); laminated cards with selected two- and three-syllable words (prepare from list, p. 115); water-based markers or highlighters

Struggling learners need ample opportunity to practice this skill with long words in isolation before they will be ready to use it in other reading materials. At first, give them only words that can be dissected according to the codes on their help card. Later, they will be able to generalize the skill to words that don't exactly match these codes. Demonstrate the process as needed before giving children cards to work through on their own. For example, to break apart the word *copper:*

- Children first scan the word for letters that make one sound. They box the *er.*

- Turning to the "help card," they see that code 1 (CVC) matches the first three letters, and they write CVC under the letters *cop*. That is the end of the first word part, so they draw a vertical dissecting mark here.

- Children now look at the "help card" to find a match for the remaining letters. Code 1 (CVC) matches again, so they write CVC under the letters *per*.

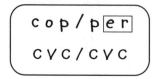

Children are now ready to read the word. They cover the second part while they focus on the first part.

- The first part, *cop*, has one vowel, so they use the short-vowel pattern (Phonics Skill 5) to read the word part *cop*.

- Looking at the second word part, they use what they know about *r*-controlled vowels (Phonics Skill 10) to read *per*.

- Finally they read both word parts together: *copper.*

By a similar process, they would use a combination of boxing letters along with codes 1, 2, and 3 to break apart and read words such as *platter, rather,* and *invent.*

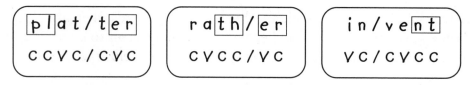

Children should keep their "help card" handy whenever they are reading as an aid to dissecting long, unfamiliar words. They should also have scrap paper on which to write and dissect long words until they are able to work through the entire process mentally.

While children will encounter words that don't quite fit the codes, the "help card" is still a good starting place that can help struggling readers begin to see shorter, more readable parts of long words.

• DAILY R-T-P •

Long-word decoding requires considerable practice, especially for struggling learners. Continue to use the R-T-P method of daily reviews for teaching and reviewing this skill.

LONG WORDS TO DECODE

blossom	enjoy	magnetic	practical	stutter
bottom	explain	manners	principal	success
bumper	export	master	problem	supper
button	fifteen	member	public	target
chapter	habit	number	random	temper
collar	happen	perform	rather	thunder
comfort	infect	perhaps	September	tractor
common	invent	platter	servant	tunnel
consider	jackets	pockets	signal	whisper
copper	lessons	powder	sister	winter

PREFIXES UN- AND RE-

STRUCTURAL SKILL 5: In words with prefixes such as *un-* and *re-*, identify the root word and recognize how the prefix changes the meaning.

A prefix is a word part added to the beginning of a root word, giving the word a new meaning. We first teach prefixes as a word-building activity; then we reverse the process and have children dissect words with prefixes, looking for clues to meaning.

To help children recognize common prefixes and distinguish them from other word groups, we keep a cumulative list of prefixes and their meanings posted in the classroom. We start our list with the prefixes *un-* and *re-*, adding other prefixes as we teach them. Children can easily refer to this list when they aren't sure if a particular word part is a prefix.

The techniques we suggest here for dissecting and reading words with *un-* and *re-* can be extended to other prefixes, including *dis-* (not), *in-* (not), *non-* (not), *pre-* (before), *mis-* (wrong), and so forth.

Word Building with Prefixes

Materials   Laminated list of definitions for words with the prefixes *un-* and *re-*, each followed by a blank (prepare from list, p. 116); water-based markers

For this technique, you should have posted for reference your cumulative list of prefixes and their meanings, which at this time will show only *un-* and *re-*.

Give children the laminated list of written definitions for words with the prefixes *un-* and *re-*. For each listed item:

- Children read the definition (for example, *not happy*).

- They underline the word that means the same as the prefix *un-* or *re-* (in this example, *not*), and box the root word (in this example, *happy*).

- They then write the new word, prefix + root (in this example, *unhappy*).

Word building is a kinesthetic and visual technique. It also improves comprehension. Because children start with a definition and use that information to choose the correct prefix, they are thinking actively about the word meanings.

Definitions for Word Building with Prefixes

1. count again _____

2. not covered _____

3. not happy _____

4. wind again _____

5. name again _____

6. not folded _____

7. write again _____

8. read again _____

9. not safe _____

10. paint again _____

11. not locked _____

12. plant again _____

13. not tied _____

14. not true _____

15. not fair _____

Word Dissecting with Prefixes

Materials   Laminated list of words with prefixes *un-* and *re-*, each followed by a blank (prepare from list below); water-based markers

In this technique, a reversal of word building, children dissect words into parts and look for prefixes that may offer meaning clues.

- Give children a list of words with the prefixes *un-* and *re-*.

- To dissect these words, children draw a line under the prefix and think about what it means.

- They then box the root word and think about its meaning.

- Finally, children write what the listed word means.

When children try to apply this word-dissecting skill in their reading, they need to understand that not every occurrence of the letters *un-* and *re-* at the beginning of a word represents a prefix. Examples are the words *uncle, under, united, repeat, reply,* and *reward.* Teach children that if they remove the assumed "prefix" and the remaining letters are not a word they recognize, then the word part is probably not a prefix and thus gives them no clue to word meaning.

List for Word Dissecting with Prefixes

1. recount _____

2. uncovered _____

3. unhappy _____

4. rewind _____

5. rename _____

6. unfolded _____

7. rewrite _____

8. reread _____

9. unsafe _____

10. repaint _____

11. unlocked _____

12. replant _____

13. untied _____

14. untrue _____

15. unfair _____

Reading Words with Prefixes in Sentences

Materials   Laminated sentence strips (see suggested sentences below); water-based markers

Children orally read each fill-in-the-blank sentence and think about the context clues. Each word choice includes either a root word and the same root word with a prefix added, or two words with prefixes. They circle the word that correctly completes the sentence and write it in the blank.

Sentences with Words that Have Prefixes Un- and Re-

1. The road was so _____ that the car bounced all over.
   (even, uneven)

2. A lie is something someone says that is _____.
   (true, untrue)

3. Two people were _____ and needed to go to the hospital.
   (hurt, unhurt)

4. The dog _____ the bone with dirt so no one would find it.
   (covered, uncovered)

5. After dinner I _____ the dirty dishes into the dishwasher.
   (load, unload)

6. On my birthday I get to _____ all my presents.
   (wrap, unwrap)

7. We had to _____ our garden when nothing came up.
   (plant, replant)

8. I _____ the sales clerk for the new pants I bought.
   (paid, repaid)

9. Remember to _____ the videotape before you take it back.
   (rewind, refill)

10. The clerk _____ the money to be sure it was the right amount.
    (replaced, recounted)

11. I had to _____ the light bulb because it burned out.
    (place, replace)

12. Rob _____ the bird feeder when the seeds were all gone.
    (renamed, refilled)

● DAILY R-T-P ●

Post a large list of prefixes and their meanings. Cover all prefixes that you have not yet taught, uncovering each as you teach it. For a quick, daily review, the children orally read each prefix and explain its meaning. Also present words with those prefixes; children read each word orally and explain its meaning.

Keeping a list of prefixes posted in the classroom helps the struggling reader figure out the meaning of an unknown word with a prefix.

SUFFIXES -FUL, -Y, -LESS, AND -LY

STRUCTURAL SKILL 6: In words with suffixes such as *-ful, -y, -less,* and *-ly,* identify the root word and recognize how the suffix changes the part of speech.

A suffix is a word part added to the end of a root word, giving the word a new function or part of speech. For example, the noun *meat* becomes an adjective when we add the suffix *-less;* the adjective *quick* becomes an adverb when we add the suffix *-ly.*

When children encounter an unknown word in their reading, they won't always recognize the final word part as a suffix. To help them, we post a cumulative list of common suffixes and their meanings, similar to the list of prefixes. We begin with *-ful, -y, -less,* and *-ly,* and add additional suffixes as we teach them. When children aren't sure if a final word part is a suffix, they can refer to the posted list.

Children need to understand that adding suffixes to root words changes the part of speech. Adding *-ful* turns words into either adjectives or, in the case of amount, into nouns (*cupful, spoonful, handful*); adding *-y* and *-less* turns words into adjectives, and adding *-ly* usually creates adverbs.

You may need to do some teaching or reteaching of the parts of speech in conjunction with these suffixes. This is best done with sentences in which the words are presented in a clear context. Struggling learners with limited oral vocabularies or English skills may have difficulty using words with suffixes correctly.

As with prefixes, we teach suffixes first as a word-building activity. Through this hands-on process, children quickly come to recognize that words with suffixes are really root words with added parts. This gives them the structural analysis skills they need for the word-dissecting activities, which prepare them to encounter words with suffixes in their reading.

Word Building with Suffixes

Materials   Laminated sets of root-word cards and, for each student pair, four laminated suffix cards (*-ful, -y, -less, -ly*). All cards must be color-coded, using colored card stock. Root-word cards are colored according to the lists (p. 121), and suffix cards are colored as follows:

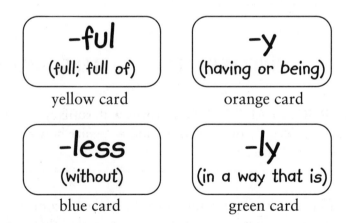

-ful (full; full of)	-y (having or being)
yellow card	orange card
-less (without)	-ly (in a way that is)
blue card	green card

This is a visual, kinesthetic, and auditory technique that involves building words by adding suffixes to given root words.

Children work in pairs. Each pair has four sets of laminated root-word cards plus the four suffix cards. They build new words by placing a suffix card to the right of a root-word card, always using only cards with matching colors. While some mismatched cards will form real words, others do not, and we have structured the activity this way to ensure that children build only real words. For example:

- One child places the yellow suffix card *-ful* to the right of the yellow root-word card *thought*.

- That child reads aloud the new word, *thoughtful,* and explains that it means *full of thought*.

- The child's partner then builds a different word with the same suffix, reads it, and explains its meaning.

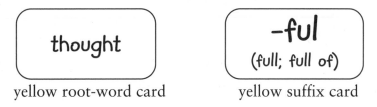

thought	-ful
	(full; full of)
yellow root-word card	yellow suffix card

Children continue to take turns until they have built and read all cards in the yellow set. They continue the activity until they have used all four root-word card sets.

ROOT WORDS FOR WORD-BUILDING CARDS

Yellow Cards	Orange Cards	Blue Cards	Green Cards
arm	boss	care	brave
care	chew	cloud	bright
cheer	chill	cord	cruel
color	cloud	end	kind
cup	dust	fear	loud
fear	fuzz	harm	neat
forget	grass	help	proud
hand	hill	home	quick
harm	leak	hope	quiet
help	mess	rest	sad
hope	rain	seed	safe
pain	rock	sleep	slow
play	salt	sleeve	smooth
spoon	sleep	spot	soft
thank	snow	thank	sweet
thought	soap	thought	tight
use	squeak	use	wild
waste	storm	wire	wise

Word Dissecting with Suffixes

Materials   Laminated cards for words with suffixes (prepare from list below); water-based markers

Dissecting words with suffixes gets children to look for clues that indicate meaning and helps them internalize this structural analysis skill. Children work in pairs with the set of laminated word cards, following this procedure:

- Children in each pair take turns choosing a card from the set.

- The child who chooses the card uses a water-based marker to draw a line under the suffix and to box the root word.

- The same child then explains the word's meaning.

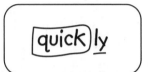 For example, one child chooses the card for *quickly*. After underlining the *-ly* and boxing the word *quick*, the child explains that the word means "in a way that is quick."

Partners continue to take turns until they have read and explained the meanings of all the cards.

WORDS WITH SUFFIXES

armful	bossy	careless	bravely
careful	chewy	cloudless	brightly
cheerful	chilly	cordless	cruelly
colorful	cloudy	endless	friendly
cupful	dusty	fearless	kindly
fearful	fuzzy	harmless	loudly
forgetful	grassy	helpless	neatly
handful	hilly	homeless	proudly
harmful	leaky	hopeless	quickly
helpful	messy	restless	quietly
hopeful	rainy	seedless	sadly
painful	rocky	sleepless	safely
playful	salty	sleeveless	slowly
spoonful	sleepy	spotless	smoothly
thankful	snowy	thankless	softly
thoughtful	soapy	thoughtless	tightly
useful	squeaky	useless	wildly
wasteful	stormy	wireless	wisely

Post a large cumulative list of suffixes and their meanings. Cover all suffixes that you have not yet taught, uncovering each as you teach it. For a quick, daily review, the children orally read each suffix and explain its meaning.

Also present words with those suffixes. Children read each word orally and explain its meaning. Keeping a list of suffixes posted in the classroom helps the struggling reader figure out the meaning of an unknown word with a suffix.

Reading Words with Suffixes in Sentences

Materials   Laminated sentence strips (see suggested sentences below); water-based markers

Children orally read each fill-in-the-blank sentence and think about the context clues. Each word choice includes two different words with suffixes. Children picture in their minds what the sentence is about and use context clues to help them decide which word fits the sentence. They then circle the correct word and write it in the blank.

Sentences with Words That Have Suffixes

1. The rabbit ran very _____ because the dog was chasing it.
   (quickly, grassy)

2. When the nurse gave me a shot in my arm, it was very _____.
   (painful, armful)

3. Our house is _____ because my dad loves to clean.
   (spotless, quietly)

4. Leaving things on the steps is _____. Someone might trip.
   (careless, grateful)

5. Sending flowers to a sick person is a _____ thing to do.
   (thankless, thoughtful)

6. The singer in the show was wearing a _____ red dress.
   (fearful, colorful)

7. Our drive to Florida was so long that it seemed _____.
   (swiftly, endless)

8. Tim is a very _____ boy who always smiles at everyone.
   (cheerful, useless)

9. Jenny walked _____ to the stage to get her award.
   (loudly, proudly)

10. You need to wear your raincoat and boots on a _____ day.
    (rainy, brightly)

11. A pencil is _____ if it has no point.
    (useless, careless)

12. Be _____ when you cross the street. Always look both ways.
    (forgetful, careful)

13. Jason played _____ when his sister was taking a nap.
    (quietly, quickly)

14. These chips make me thirsty because they are very _____.
    (salty, useful)

15. I like to use a _____ phone that I can take outside.
    (harmless, cordless)

Connecting Suffixes to Parts of Speech

Materials   Laminated fill-in-the-blank sentence strips (see suggested sentences below); water-based markers

If you have struggling learners who have trouble correctly using words with suffixes, this activity can help them link certain suffixes with particular parts of speech.

- When they see the suffixes *-ful*, *-y*, and *-less*, the words are usually adjectives—words that describe nouns or pronouns.

- When they see the suffix *-ly*, the words are usually adverbs—words that describe verbs by telling how something is done.

Present fill-in-the-blank sentences with clear context clues to help children decide whether to use the root word or the root word plus a suffix. Once they have chosen the word that makes sense in the sentence, children orally "prove" that the words with suffixes are either adjectives or adverbs. With markers, they draw an arrow from the word with the suffix to the word it describes, and explain how they know.

SAMPLE SENTENCE STRIPS

Mary is <u>helpful</u> when she washes the dishes for her mom. (help, helpful)

The boy ran <u>quickly</u> and won the race. (quick, quickly)

Sentences for Connecting Suffixes to Parts of Speech

1. The _____ girl brought flowers to her grandmother.
     (thoughtful, thought)

2. The _____ man ran into the burning house to save the family inside.
     (fearless, fear)

3. Tom limped home _____ after he hurt his leg playing soccer.
          (sadly, sad)

4. The _____ puppy jumped up and down with the ball.
    (play, playful)

5. I cleaned up my _____ room to surprise my mom.
    (mess, messy)

6. I like to buy _____ grapes because they are easier to eat.
    (seedless, seed)

7. To ride your bike _____, you must always wear a helmet.
    (safely, safe)

8. Tim was very tired today because he had a _____ night.
    (sleep, sleepless)

9. The actors spoke _____ so everyone could hear them.
    (loudly, loud)

10. They washed the dog in a big tub of _____ water.
    (soap, soapy)

• DAILY R-T-P •

Use the last row of boxes on the Reading Tools chart (p. 49) to review three ways good readers figure out unknown words.
- With the "long-word help card," they think of the codes on the card, match a code to the letters in the word, and break the long word into smaller parts.
- Finding the root word, or the word that was there before a prefix or suffix was added, helps children figure out unknown words.
- "Look at the other words for clues" reminds children that when they come to an unknown word, they can look at the words around it for meaning clues to help them figure it out.

Comprehension

Comprehension and active thinking must be taught and practiced if children are to become successful readers.

Comprehension, or the ability to understand a written text, is not something that comes automatically to struggling learners. It is a facet of reading that we must begin to teach when children first start to read words, and continue to teach and refine as they progress to more difficult reading material.

For struggling learners, comprehension is often lost while they are focused on phonics and structural analysis skills. With so much attention needed just to figure out individual words, these children lose the bigger picture.

To help with comprehension, we teach struggling learners to follow a two-step process: (1) think about what the words mean, and (2) picture them in their minds. We call this process *active thinking*.

When readers think constantly about what the words mean and make mental pictures, the words they are reading look right, sound right, and make sense. Readers who use active thinking will self-correct when words *don't* look right, sound right, or make sense. Learning the active-thinking process results in improved comprehension.

Active thinking underlies all nine of the comprehension skills we help children practice:

- **Comprehension Skill 1: Recalling Details** Part of understanding the text is being able to recall details about it: *Who* was it about? *What* were they doing? *Where* were they? *When* was it happening?

- **Comprehension Skill 2: Sequence** Events happen in a certain order. Readers who comprehend are able to follow and reconstruct that sequence.

- **Comprehension Skill 3: Word Referents** To eliminate repetition, all writers use word referents, including pronouns, as substitutes for key words in a story. To understand what they are reading, children need to be able to connect these referents to the words they stand for.

- **Comprehension Skill 4: Context Clues** In order to read and understand unfamiliar words, children need to pay attention to the surrounding words for clues.

- **Comprehension Skill 5: Predicting Outcomes** Asking children to make sensible predictions encourages them to think about and picture what they are reading.

- **Comprehension Skill 6: Main Idea** Identifying the main idea helps children put together all the details to understand the larger picture.

- **Comprehension Skill 7: Inference/Drawing Conclusions** Children extend their active thinking to "read between the lines" when they understand things that are implied rather than explicitly stated in text.

- **Comprehension Skill 8: Character Traits** Paying attention to how characters are acting and what they are saying helps children make inferences about things that are not directly stated in the text.

- **Comprehension Skill 9: Cause and Effect** Children are better able to make sense of a sequence of events when they can identify the likely cause of an event, or the effect of someone's actions.

Many of these nine skills overlap. For example, being able to identify main idea or to predict what happens next or to make inferences from the text are all dependent on recognizing and recalling the details of the reading passage. Similarly, recognizing character traits from what the characters do or say also involves making inferences; recognizing cause and effect is supported by children's understanding of sequence.

The techniques in this chapter simply offer a way to focus on particular aspects of comprehension while children are working to put together all their reading skills.

Struggling learners need both teacher-directed instruction and lots of practice with active thinking and comprehension skills. Although we emphasize reading sentences for understanding even while children are working on new phonics skills (chapters 1–3), we specifically shift the focus to these nine comprehension skills as soon as children are familiar with all the early-reading and first-grade phonics and vocabulary skills (chapters 1 and 2).

For each comprehension skill, we suggest two techniques: one for introducing the skill at a simple level, often with one or just a few sentences;

the other for extending the skill to longer passages. In each case, we include reading material with a loosely controlled vocabulary for both the first-grade and second-grade levels, which we call Level 1 and Level 2.

Material for Level 1 assumes that children have mastered the skills presented in chapters 1 and 2, while material for Level 2 assumes mastery of the chapter 3 skills. Children use context clues to help them read any words with spelling patterns they have not yet learned.

Regardless of the technique we are using, we always move through the following three steps in our teaching:

- **Establish prior knowledge.** If children are to understand what they read, they need some prior experience with the events they are reading about. Our role as teachers is to assess what children already know and fill in the gaps in their knowledge when the material contains unfamiliar vocabulary, unfamiliar settings, or unfamiliar events. It is like being a tour guide, showing, explaining, and helping the children make sense of what they will be reading.

  This step must always be done *before* the reading begins. It is especially important for children who speak English as a second language. When stories are illustrated, one way to provide prior knowledge is to let children "walk" through the stories by looking at the pictures, then take turns putting the pictures into words. When children first tell the story themselves in this way, the stage is set for them to use active thinking as they read.

- **Follow up with teacher-directed instruction.** For introducing and extending each comprehension skill, we rely on oral questioning, feedback, and continual reminders to children to use active thinking and visualization while they read. In this way we ensure that children stay involved in the reading material and genuinely understand what the words are saying.

- **Give children uninterrupted time to reread for fluency.** After teacher-directed instruction, children need the chance to reread the material, without interruption. The goal is to read with understanding while the words flow smoothly and correctly. This rereading increases fluency, improves comprehension, and boosts children's confidence. Rereading for fluency is a positive way to end a reading session.

Please keep in mind that the materials in these pages are only a starting point for your classroom work; you will of course continue to extend the work on comprehension and active thinking to any reading materials you are using with your struggling learners.

RECALLING DETAILS

COMPREHENSION SKILL 1: Recognize and recall details that tell who, what, where, and when.

Struggling learners tend to read by word calling, never actively thinking about what the words mean. These children are passive readers; they don't create mental images of *who* is in the story, *what* they are doing, where they are, and *when* it is taking place. As a result, they can't remember these details when the teacher asks questions afterward.

Children who do create mental images as they read are generally able to recall the details of *who, what, when,* and *where.* That's why we emphasize the active-thinking process for the struggling learner. Through active thinking and visualization, the children should feel as if they are physically involved in the stories. When that happens, they usually have no difficulty recalling story details.

Introducing the Skill: Recalling Details in Sentences

Materials   Who-What-Where-When board (prepare on poster board or chart paper, as illustrated); laminated lists of sentences, written on cards or on chart paper (prepare from lists, pp. 131–132)

When children are reading sentences, each sentence is a miniature story. Like a longer story, a sentence may tell about someone doing something, and where or when that person was doing it.

Display the Who-What-Where-When board and distribute or post the lists of sentences. Before children begin reading, explain that you are going to be asking them to remember *who* is in the story that each sentence is telling, *what* they are doing, *where* they are, and *when* something happened.

For example, children will read in unison, "The small white dog jumped up and down on the rug this morning." If they are creating mental images as they read, they will be able to tell you that *who* is "the small white dog," *what* is "jumped up and down," *where* is "on the rug," and *when* is "this morning." You record these details on the board under the appropriate headings.

As needed, explain that *who* won't always be a person—it may sometimes be a thing. Children should also understand that some sentence-stories may not include all four details, and some may have more than one *who, what, when,* or *where.*

Tap a steady beat while the children read orally in unison, one word at a time, to the beat. Remind children to create mental images as they read. If they struggle with any words, have them make their best guess and ask, "Does it look right? Does it sound right? Does it make sense?" These questions help children focus on context clues and keep them thinking about what the words mean.

WHO-WHAT-WHERE-WHEN BOARD

Who?	What?
Where?	
When?	

Recalling Details: Sentences for Level 1

1. Tim can dip his hot feet in the lake after lunch.

2. Mom twists Pam's hair into a long braid every day.

3. After the game, Joe and Pete fell down on the wet grass.

4. Jim fried six fish for us to eat for lunch at noon.

5. I closed the gate to keep my dog locked in the yard.

6. Today I will try not to trip over the hose on the grass.

7. I found my new bike around the block.

8. My dog sat on the mat and ate a bone all day long.

9. The glass broke when it fell off the shelf.

10. Every day Jake wakes up at six o'clock.

Recalling Details: Sentences for Level 2

1. Josh took his fishing pole and some hooks to the lake before dinner. He hoped he could catch a large trout.

2. My sister and I have chores to do after school. My job is to sweep the kitchen floor, and her job is to walk the dog.

3. I looked in the tool chest to find the hammer and a nail. I used the nail to hang a pretty picture over my bed.

4. The large, mean dog growls every time someone rings the doorbell.

5. All the birds fly south in the winter because it is too cold in the north.

6. Tonight we will go to sleep early because we are very tired.

7. Vince was out of breath after he jogged five miles this morning.

8. Dawn and Mandy enjoy playing soccer every Saturday.

9. The ground is still moist because it rained for a long time last night.

10. Everybody in our class is going to the zoo on Monday afternoon.

Extending the Skill: Recalling Details in Stories

Materials   Laminated story sheets (prepare on tagboard; see samples at two reading levels, pp. 133–134); Who-What-Where-When board

Children orally read a story. Ask questions like those following each sample story to promote active thinking and visualization and to draw children into the setting of the story. Remind them, "Think about what the words mean, and picture them in your mind."

After reading, children recall the details while you write them on the Who-What-Where-When board under the proper headings. Stories vary in complexity, but since more events occur in a story than in a sentence, the various sections of the board will likely have more than one listing.

Recalling Details: Story for Level 1

One spring day Jack sat by the old oak tree. He wanted to be out of the hot sun, so he sat in the shade. As he rested, he looked up in the branches of the tree. He saw a nest with three white eggs in it.

One of the eggs had a small hole in it. While he watched, he saw a beak poke out of the hole in the shell. Then the shell broke open and there sat a brown baby bird. The baby bird was too little to fly away.

Jack did not pick up the bird. He knew that would scare it. He just rested under the old oak tree with a smile on his face. If he waited, maybe he would see two more baby birds.

Teacher-Directed Questions

1. Who is in the story? (Jack and a baby bird)

2. What happened in the story? (Jack was sitting by the old oak tree. He saw a nest with three eggs. He watched one of the eggs hatch. Jack did not touch the baby bird. He waited to see if the other two eggs would hatch.)

3. Where does the story take place? (outside by an old oak tree)

4. When does the story take place? (one spring day)

Recalling Details: Story for Level 2

Carissa lived near the park where she could play baseball. She didn't want to take dance lessons or flute lessons. She didn't like to play with dolls. She only wanted to play baseball with the boys in the neighborhood.

One Saturday she put her sneakers on her feet and ran to the park. She knew all the boys would be there, getting ready to play baseball. When she arrived at the park, she asked the boys if she could join them in their game.

At first, the boys laughed at her and said that she probably couldn't hit the ball. She begged them to give her just one chance. Her first time at bat, she hit the ball into left field and ran to second base. The boys were shocked that she had so much power and could run so quickly. Carissa's heart pounded, and she was excited because she hit the ball so hard.

The next time she was at bat, Carissa hit a single and ran to first base. Once again, the boys were surprised that she could play so well. During the last inning of the game, Carissa caught a fly ball that ended the game. That catch helped her team win the game by one run. Now, the boys argue because they all want Carissa to be on their team!

Teacher-Directed Questions

1. Who is in the story? (Carissa and the boys in her neighborhood)

2. What happened in the story? (Carissa went to the park. She asked the boys if she could play baseball. They laughed, then agreed to give her a chance. Carissa hit and ran to second base. She hit the ball again and ran to first base. She caught a fly ball that ended the game. Her team won. All the boys want Carissa on their team.)

3. Where does the story take place? (in the park)

4. When does the story take place? (Saturday)

Comprehension

SEQUENCE

COMPREHENSION SKILL 2: Recognize and recreate the sequence
of events in a reading passage.

Recognizing the sequence of events in a story helps children make sense of
what they are reading. One clue to the order of events is the use of "signal"
words, or words that indicate time and order, such as *then, next, before, after,
finally,* and *in the morning.* If struggling learners ignore these signal words and
focus only on the remaining words, they may have a mental picture of *what* is
happening, but no sense of *when* things are happening.

A FEW SIGNAL WORDS

first	earlier	at the same time
second	later	in the morning
third	before	in the afternoon
fourth	after	at night
fifth	during	before school
sixth	next	at lunchtime
seventh	then	after school
eighth	finally	at bedtime
ninth	noon	when the sun goes down
tenth	midnight	when the sun comes up

For example, suppose children read this sentence: "Before we went
swimming, we had to clean our rooms." Struggling readers may not notice the
word *before* and will focus only on the more easily pictured words *went
swimming* and *clean our rooms.* When asked, "What happened first?" these
children may answer, "We went swimming," simply because that action
appears first in the sentence.

Because a single word can change the order of events, children need to pay
close attention to these sequence markers. Thinking about the signal words as
they read helps them understand that time is passing and enables them to
picture the sequence of events.

Introducing the Skill: Sequencing by Signal Words

Materials   Sets of laminated signal-word story cards, three to five cards per set, prepared on half sheets of tagboard (see illustrated examples below, and suggested sentences, pp. 137–138); water-based markers

    Children work with a set of laminated signal-word story cards, labeled on one side with the title of the story.

- Children read the title, then turn the cards over to read the sentence on each card.

- Using water-based markers, children circle the signal words that indicate time and order. Actively thinking about these signal words helps children create mental images of the sequence of events.

- Children then arrange the cards in the correct sequence.

- To reinforce comprehension, have children illustrate each sentence on the lower part of the card.

- Finally, have children orally reread the sentences on all the cards in the set, in order, checking to make sure that the sequence makes sense.

SET OF SIGNAL-WORD STORY CARDS

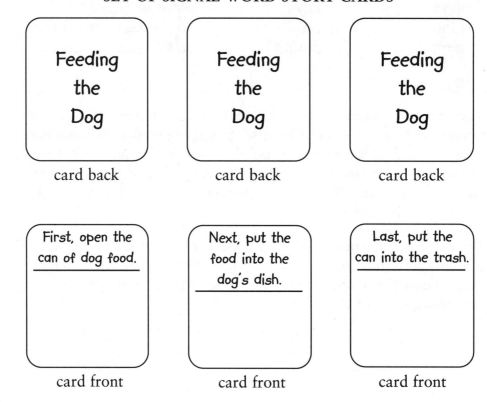

Feeding the Dog

card back

Feeding the Dog

card back

Feeding the Dog

card back

First, open the can of dog food.

card front

Next, put the food into the dog's dish.

card front

Last, put the can into the trash.

card front

Comprehension

Sequence: Signal-Word Story Cards for Level 1

Title (card backs): *Getting Ready for Bed*

Sentences:
First, Tim brushes his teeth and washes his face.
Next, he puts on his pj's.
Last, Tim gets into bed.

Title (card backs): *Walking the Dog*

Sentences:
Before I take the dog for a walk, I put on his leash.
After that, I walk him down the street.
Then, we go back home.

Title (card backs): *Going to the Bus Stop*

Sentences:
At nine o'clock, I grab my book bag.
Next, I walk to the bus stop.
Finally, I get on the bus.

Title (card backs): *What I Do at Sundown*

Sentences:
Every night when the sun goes down, I go home.
Now, it is time to eat my big meal of the day.
After that, I do my homework and then go to bed.

Title (card backs): *Flying a Kite*

Sentences:
Before lunch, Molly saw the wind blowing the trees.
She ate her lunch fast because she wanted to fly her kite.
After lunch, Molly ran outside to fly her kite.

Title (card backs): *Going Skating*

Sentences:
On Monday Sam wanted to skate, but it rained.
On Tuesday before school, the sun was bright.
When he got home on Tuesday, Sam went skating.

Title (card backs): *Going Fishing*

Sentences:
When the sun comes up, Dad and Tom plan to go fishing.
Before they leave home, they get their fishing rods and bait.
First they must drive to the lake.
One hour later, Tom pulls a big fish into the boat.

Title (card backs): *Taking Care of a Cut*

Sentences:
I cut my leg when I fell down in the street.
Then I ran into the house to wash off the cut.
After I washed my leg, I put a bandage on the cut.

Sequence: Signal-Word Story Cards for Level 2

Title (card backs): *Eating Breakfast*

Sentences:
In the morning, I go into the kitchen to fix my breakfast.
First, I get out a blue bowl, some milk, and the cereal.
Next, I pour some cereal and milk into the blue bowl.
Finally, I can eat my cereal.

Title (card backs): *Cleaning My Glasses*

Sentences:
When I first put on my glasses, I saw that they were dirty.
After I saw how dirty they were, I took them to the sink.
Next, I washed them off with soap and water.
I can finally see through my clean glasses.

Title (card backs): *The Swings in the Park*

Sentences:
This afternoon, I want to play on the swings in the park.
Before I leave home I put on my play clothes.
Then I ride my bike to the park.
At the park, I jump onto a swing and fly high into the air.

Title (card backs): *Playing Catch with My Dog*

Sentences:
I get a ball and take my dog into the backyard.
Then, I throw the ball to my dog.
He runs after the ball with all his might.
He catches it in his mouth.
Finally, he runs back with the ball so I can throw it again.

Title (card backs):	*Going Swimming*
Sentences:	Before I leave, I put on my swim suit and grab a towel.
	As I am leaving, Mom tells me not to forget the sunscreen.
	I go back inside the house to get the sunscreen.
	When I get to the pool, I rub the sunscreen on.
	Finally I jump into the pool.

Title (card backs):	*Buying Groceries*
Sentences:	Dad and I get into the car and drive to the grocery store.
	We walk into the store and get a cart.
	Next, we walk around and put the things we need into the cart.
	When the cart is full, we get in line and Dad pays for the groceries.
	Finally Dad drives home and I help him put the groceries away.

Extending the Skill: Finding Sequence in Stories

Materials   Laminated story sheets (prepare on tagboard; see sample stories, pp. 140–142); water-based markers

Children read the story and circle the signal words as they read. Focusing on signal words helps children place themselves in the story and better understand the sequence of events. After reading, ask questions to help children create mental images of the story as they recall the sequence of events.

A little white dog played hide and seek with a big brown goat. First, the goat went to hide while the dog counted to 50 with his eyes closed. Then, the dog went to find the goat. Where was she?

The first place the little dog looked was under the big pine tree. The goat was not there.

The next place the dog looked was in the tall grass near the shed. She was not in the tall grass.

The last place the little dog looked was inside the shed. He opened the door to the shed and saw the goat. Just as the dog was going to tag her, the goat ran out the door.

The dog chased the goat around and around. At last the little dog tagged the goat. They liked to play this game. When it was over, they were tired and hot from running around in the sun.

Teacher-Directed Questions

1. Who hid first? (the goat)

2. What did the dog do while the goat was hiding? (counted with his eyes closed)

3. What happened next? (The dog went to look for the goat.)

4. Where did the dog look first? (under the big pine tree)

5. Where did the dog look next? (in the tall grass near the shed)

6. Where did the dog look last? (inside the shed)

7. What happened next? (The dog opened the door and saw the goat.)

8. What happened when the dog tried to tag the goat? (The goat ran out the door.)

9. What happened next? (The dog chased the goat and tagged her.)

10. When were the dog and goat tired and hot? (when the game was over)

Sequence: Story for Level 2

One spring morning, the loud ringing of my telephone woke me up. My cousin Tyler was calling to ask if he could come visit me. Since I live near the zoo, Tyler wanted me to help him with his school project. He wanted to take pictures of some animals. I said that I would be happy to help him.

The next morning, Tyler came on the bus. After I met the bus, we went out for lunch. That afternoon, we went to the zoo. Tyler took his mom's camera to the zoo.

First, Tyler took pictures of the monkeys swinging on long ropes. Then, we went to see the elephants. They were playing with watermelons. Tyler took a picture of one elephant smashing a watermelon, then eating it.

Next we saw a baby giraffe standing next to its mother. When the mother giraffe licked the baby's forehead, Tyler quickly snapped a picture. Finally, we stopped at the tigers' den. The two tigers were playing with a large striped ball. One tiger used his paw to slap the ball to the other tiger. Tyler was lucky because he was able to take a wonderful picture of them playing with the ball.

When we left the zoo, we took the film to a one-hour photo store. The clerk at the store told us that our pictures would be ready in an hour. While the pictures were being made, we went to the ice cream store for ice cream cones and drinks.

When we were finished with our snack, it was time to pick up the pictures. The pictures turned out perfectly, and Tyler knew that his project would be fantastic.

Teacher-Directed Questions

1. What happened first? (the phone rang)

2. When did Tyler arrive? (the next morning)

3. How did he get to my house? (by bus)

4. What happened after I met Tyler's bus? (We went to lunch.)

5. When did we go to the zoo? (that afternoon)

6. Name the animals, in order, as we saw them. (monkeys, elephants, giraffes, and tigers)

7. What were the tigers doing in the picture Tyler took? (playing with a ball)

8. What did we do when we left the zoo? (We went to the one-hour photo store.)

9. What happened at the same time that we were having ice cream cones and drinks? (The pictures were being made.)

10. What did we do after we ate our snack? (picked up the pictures)

WORD REFERENTS

COMPREHENSION SKILL 3: Recognize a word referent as a substitute for another word or words.

Word referents are words that stand for or refer to other words in the text. They include both personal and demonstrative pronouns *(he, she, they, them, him, hers,* and so forth) as well as nouns such as *here* and *there.* We use these words in writing to avoid repeating the same nouns over and over again, making the text more concise and less cumbersome.

For struggling learners, the difficulty usually lies in recognizing who or what the word referents stand for. For those with limited oral language skills or English as a second language, the gender of personal pronouns *(he/she, his/hers, him/her)* can sometimes be confusing as well.

WORD REFERENTS

Singular

I	my/mine	me	this
you	your/yours	you	that
he	his	him	
she	her/hers	her	here
it	its	it	there
who	whose	whom	

Plural

you	your/yours	you	these
we	our/ours	us	those
they	their/theirs	them	

We ask children to use active thinking and visualization—to think about what the words mean and picture them in their minds—to determine the meaning of these substitute words. For example, "Tom went to the river on Wednesday. *He* liked watching the swans *there.*" *He* and *there* are word referents. Through active thinking, children should be able to connect *he* to the name *Tom* and *there* to the place *river.*

Before practicing this skill, children should have prior knowledge of word referents and their usage, including which pronouns are singular and plural, and which are specifically male and female. You might post a list of word referents to help children identify and become familiar with them.

Introducing the Skill: Word Referents in Sentences

Materials   Laminated sentence strips with word referents underlined or omitted (see suggested sentences below); water-based markers

Children working at level 1 orally read sentences in which the word referent is underlined. They determine who or what the word referent stands for by thinking about and picturing what the words mean. Using water-based markers, they circle the word or words that the word referent stands for and draw an arrow from the referent to the circled words. For example:

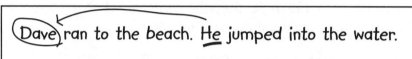

On the sentence strips for level 2, the word referent is omitted. Children orally read the sentence and decide which word referent makes sense, then fill in the blank. It may be helpful for struggling learners to draw an arrow from the inserted word referent to the word or words to which it refers.

Word Referents: Sentences for Level 1

1. Bill and I ran all the way home. Now <u>we</u> are very tired.

2. Ann and Sue like to sing. <u>They</u> always sing together.

3. I got a skateboard for my birthday. Let me show you <u>my</u> skateboard.

4. The doghouse needs to be painted. <u>It</u> used to be white.

5. This old book belongs to Tim. He takes good care of <u>his</u> books.

6. Mom and I made up a new game. We named <u>our</u> game "Whiz Kids."

7. Zack has a new bike. <u>He</u> rides it a lot.

8. Rose has a large sandbox in her yard. <u>She</u> likes to build castles in the sand.

9. My friends want to buy a new TV. <u>Their</u> TV is not working.

10. Mom will fix lunch for Dan and Sue. She will give <u>them</u> ham and cheese.

Word Referents: Sentences for Level 2

1. Karl can go very fast on his skateboard. _____ can do a flip in the air.

2. We like to eat fish for dinner. _____ favorite kind of fish is flounder.

3. Megan and Mark are both in Mrs. Yee's reading class. _____ like to go there because she helps them read better.

4. Tigers live in the deep, dark jungle. They search for _____ food among the trees.

5. My favorite color is blue. _____ is my mother's favorite color, too.

6. I am going to the mountains this summer. _____ cousin is coming, too.

7. The bird's nest is full of light blue eggs. The mother bird sits on _____ until they hatch.

8. My ball is stuck on the roof. How will I get _____ down?

9. These are not my boots. Sofie has some, too. They must be _____.

10. Jenny gazes up at the moon from her bedroom window. _____ would like to go there someday.

Extending the Skill: Word Referents in Stories

Materials   Laminated story sheets (prepare on tagboard; see sample stories, pp. 146–148); highlighters

Children orally read stories and highlight the word referents, a process that gets children to think about who or what the word referent stands for. Ask questions like those provided to encourage active thinking and visualization. After directed instruction and questioning, allow children time to reread the stories for fluency. Struggling readers increase their comprehension as well as their fluency through this rereading process.

Word Referents: Story for Level 1

Once there were two little bugs. They loved to play in the tall green grass. They were funny little bugs who liked to hop up and down all day long. They never got tired of doing that. Boys and girls would stand around and watch the two little bugs put on a show. They always laughed and clapped when the show was over.

One day two boys tried to put on their own show. They hopped up and down in the tall grass, but this was not very funny. Hopping up and down only made them tired. It also made their pants turn green from grass stains! When the boys saw the stains, they knew it was time to go home. Next time they will just go back and laugh at the funny, hopping bugs.

Teacher-Directed Questions

1. Find the sentence, "They loved to play in the tall green grass." To whom does *they* refer? (the two bugs)

2. Find the sentence, "They never got tired of doing that." To whom does *they* refer? (the two bugs) To what does *that* refer? (hopping up and down on the grass)

3. Find the sentence, "They always laughed and clapped when the show was over." To whom does *they* refer? (the boys and girls)

4. Find the sentence, "They hopped up and down in the tall grass, but this was not very funny." To what does *this* refer? (the boys' hopping up and down)

5. Find the sentence, "Hopping up and down only made them tired." To whom does *them* refer? (the two boys)

6. Find the sentence, "It also made their pants turn green from grass stains!" *Their* pants means whose pants? (the two boys' pants)

Word Referents: Story for Level 2

Little Lester was four years old. He always dreamed that someday he would fly to the moon, or maybe the stars. One day, Little Lester saw a magic mule flying over the trees and across the sky. He yelled to the mule, "That looks like fun! Please give me a ride."

Being magic, the mule could talk as well as fly. He said, "Of course you may have a ride, but it is very cold today. I'm afraid you will freeze."

"I can fix that," Little Lester cried out. He ran home as fast as he could. He was just putting on his new coat when he heard the magic mule calling his name. The mule called, "Hurry, Lester, so we can start our ride."

Little Lester quickly ran outside. The mule said, "Jump on my back, and I will take you wherever you want to go." Little Lester climbed onto the mule's back. His heart was pounding a hundred beats a minute as they took off into the cold, blue sky.

Many boys and girls were in the park, playing on the swings and slides. When they looked up, they saw a strange sight in the sky. One girl screamed, "Lester! What are you doing up there on that strange mule?"

Little Lester answered in a strong voice, "We are going to the moon, or maybe the stars!" Then Little Lester waved good-bye, and he and the magic mule flew off on the ride of their lives.

Teacher-Directed Questions

1. Find the sentence, "He yelled to the mule, 'That looks like fun! Please give me a ride.'" To whom does *he* refer? (Little Lester) To what does *that* refer? (flying over the trees and across the sky) To whom does *me* refer? (Little Lester)

2. Find the sentence, "Of course you may have a ride, but it is very cold today." To whom does *you* refer? (Little Lester)

3. Find the sentence, "He was just putting on his new coat when he heard the magic mule calling his name." *His* coat refers to whose coat? (Little Lester's)

4. Find the sentence, "The mule called, 'Hurry, Lester, so we can start our ride.'" *Our* ride refers to whose ride? (Little Lester and the mule's)

5. Find the sentence, "The mule said, 'Jump on my back, and I will take you wherever you want to go.'" To whom does *you* refer? (Little Lester)

6. Find the sentence, "When they looked up, they saw a strange sight in the sky." To whom does *they* refer? (the boys and girls in the park)

7. Find the sentence, "What are you doing up there on that strange mule?" To whom does *you* refer? (Little Lester)

CONTEXT CLUES

COMPREHENSION SKILL 4: Use context clues to help determine the meaning of unknown words.

Children use context clues whenever they try to figure out a word by actively thinking about the words that surround it. Once they visualize what the rest of the sentence is about, they can often figure out what word would fit in that context.

Not all children automatically search for and use context clues. Successful readers use this strategy, but struggling learners tend to "word call" without thinking about what they are saying. Faced with an unknown word, passive readers frequently make up something, even though it doesn't make sense. They do this just to end the reading process quickly.

We have already encouraged struggling readers to use context clues while they are reading sentences for their work on phonics skills. However, the skill is worth some extra attention because it is a valuable way to figure out the meaning of words that readers can decode but that are not in their speaking vocabularies. Only if they understand the individual words can children make sense of the printed page.

Using context clues means being an active thinker. Suppose your children encounter this sentence:

> The limbs and leaves of the tree were tossed all over the yard in the strong windstorm.

Some readers likely won't know the word *limb,* but the sentence is full of context clues: *leaves, tree, tossed, all over the yard, strong windstorm.* Once they picture the rest of the sentence, and place themselves in the setting, children should realize that whatever *limbs* are, they were tossed all over the yard by the wind—so maybe *limbs* means *branches.*

Examining the other words for context clues should be one of the first strategies that readers use when they hit a roadblock in reading.

During your work on using context clues, just as with other comprehension skills, struggling readers will need many reminders to practice active thinking. For a visual and kinesthetic reminder, teach children to follow your lead with two motions: point to your head as a reminder to think about what the words mean, then either pretend to draw a picture or "turn on the television" in their minds to picture the words.

Refer to the box for other ways to trigger active thinking. We use all of them, at different times, because our struggling learners respond to a variety of methods and require many practice sessions before they have internalized the skill.

Teacher-Directed Ways to Trigger Active Thinking

- Have children role-play what they read.

- Ask, "What does that mean? Does that make sense?"

- Have children retell the story in their own words.

- Ask, "Do you feel like you are right there in the story?"

- Ask, "How did you figure out that unknown word?"

- Have children substitute synonyms to explain the meanings of difficult words.

Introducing the Skill: Context Clues in Sentences

Materials   Laminated sentence strips (see suggested sentences below); water-based markers

Children orally read sentences with either blanks to fill in (first-grade level) or underlined words (second-grade level).

- For level 1, children circle the context clues in the sentence, think about what they mean, and visualize what is going on. Circling the context clues leads struggling learners into active thinking and also helps them "prove" their answers. They then choose the word that best fits, circle it, and write it in the blank.

- For level 2, children circle the context clues that help them figure out the meaning of the underlined word. They orally explain the meaning of the underlined word, using the context clues they circled to prove their answers.

After teacher-directed instruction, allow children time to reread the sentences for fluency.

Context Clues: Sentences for Level 1

1. Where did Grace leave her _____? She needs it to go to school!   (coat, cold)

2. Are you going to the store? I need some _____ for my lunch.   (chairs, cheese)

3. Please _____ your hands before you eat your lunch.   (brush, wash)

4. Pants and _____ are the same thing.   (slacks, belts)

5. Ann has a pet that swims in a tank. Her pet is a _____.   (cat, fish)

6. Pack your old books in a box and tie it with a _____.

   (bring, string)

7. Today I get my braces off my teeth. I can't wait to _____ at everyone.

   (smile, smell)

Context Clues: Sentences for Level 2

1. My brother tried to <u>conceal</u> his bad grades from Mom and Dad by hiding them in his room.

2. Our new kitten is very <u>frisky</u>. She likes to play and chase her tail and run around all day long!

3. The flower seeds that I planted last week are beginning to <u>sprout</u>. I can see the tiny green stem coming up out of the soil.

4. When my dad dropped his coffee cup, it broke into many pieces. He spent a long time picking up <u>fragments</u> of the cup.

5. In art class, I mixed some red and blue paint. After <u>blending</u> them together, I had purple paint.

6. Please do not <u>murmur</u>. I can't understand you when you speak so softly.

7. We had clam <u>chowder</u> for dinner last night. It was rainy and cold, so the warm soup tasted very good.

Extending the Skill: Context Clues in Stories

Materials   Laminated story sheets (prepare on tagboard; see sample stories, pp. 152–153); water-based markers

Children reading at the first-grade level orally read a story with blanks to be filled in from a word bank. Using active thinking, they visualize what is going on in the story and circle the clues that help them decide what word goes in each blank. They write in the words, then reread the story for fluency and to check that their answers make sense.

For work at the second-grade level, children read a story with some words underlined. They circle the context clues that help them know the meaning of those words. Remind them that context clues may be found before or after the underlined word, and sometimes in another sentence. Finally, children orally explain the meaning of the underlined words, using the circled context clues to support their answers. Following this exercise, give them a chance to reread the paragraph for fluency to improve their comprehension.

Context Clues: Story for Level 1

> **WORD BANK**
>
> home   mall   race   ice
>
> nice   bed   doll   mice

Last week my mom drove us to the big _____ where we saw many shops. We went into the pet shop to look at the white _____ with the long thin tails. The mice ran around in a glass tank. Two of them ran so fast, I think they wanted to have a _____. They were fun to watch.

After we left the pet shop, we went to get a juice drink. I asked the man to put _____ in my juice to make it cold. The man was very _____ and smiled when he gave me my glass.

Next we went to the toy shop. Mom said I could buy a _____, one that I can feed, dress, and wash. I love my new doll!

At the end of the day we went _____ to eat. Then I took my new doll to _____ with me. I needed to rest. The trip to the mall was fun, but I was very tired.

Comprehension

Context Clues: Story for Level 2

One day Michael and his father went for a ride on a train. Michael wanted to learn about the different kinds of cars and the people who worked on the train. The <u>conductor</u>, the man who collected tickets, told Michael that he would be glad to show him everything.

The first car they visited was the <u>engine</u>. This car was the one that pulls all the other cars on the train. In the engine car, Michael met the <u>engineer</u> who drove the train. Then they walked to the <u>coach</u> car where all the people were sitting. The <u>passengers</u> had to speak very loudly because the train was very noisy.

The next car was very dirty. It was the <u>mail</u> car, full of packages wrapped for mailing. Most of those <u>parcels</u> were taped to keep everything inside.

Finally, they visited the <u>caboose</u>, which is the last car on the train. The conductor who showed them around was so nice, Michael later wrote him a note to <u>convey</u> thanks for a fantastic day on the train.

PREDICTING OUTCOMES

COMPREHENSION SKILL 5: Make sensible predictions based on context clues in a reading passage.

The ability to predict outcomes is another way readers demonstrate that they understand what they are reading. Successful readers put themselves in the setting of the story through active thinking. They want to know what will happen next, and they are anxious to continue reading.

Struggling learners, on the other hand, may have difficulty anticipating what happens next because they do not actively think about what they are reading. Their minds stray from the setting and they do not feel as if they are "right there." It is difficult for them to predict, because they aren't sure what has already happened in the story.

Predicting outcomes requires children to "read between the lines," using both prior knowledge of events and details from stories to make sensible predictions. For this reason, be sure to provide background information to children who have limited experience with the subject of the story. Children may have trouble making a prediction about something that happens at a circus if they have never seen one, or about something that happens at the beach if they have never been to the ocean.

Children need to understand that their prediction does not have to be "correct," as long as it makes sense and is supported by information from the story. We teach struggling readers to use context clues and active thinking to help them make sensible predictions because whether or not their prediction is right, thinking about the possibilities keeps them engaged with the reading material.

Introducing the Skill:
Predicting Outcomes in Short-Short Stories

Materials   Laminated short-short story cards (see illustrated examples, p. 155, and suggested stories, pp. 156–158); water-based markers

Present a short-short story, written on a laminated activity card, with room for the child to illustrate the story. At the first-grade reading level, children are given three possible predictions; they circle the most sensible. At the second-grade reading level, children write their own predictions. There may be more than one right answer; any prediction is acceptable if the child can support it with details from the story.

For example, in the sample shown opposite, building a snowman is one good prediction. Others might involve sledding, throwing snowballs, or making snow angels.

During directed instruction, ask questions to help struggling learners place themselves in the setting of the story: Who is in the story? What are they doing? Where are they? When did that happen? Do you feel like you are right there in the story?

Struggling learners should orally explain their predictions and illustrations to be sure they make sense.

SAMPLE SHORT-SHORT STORY CARD FOR LEVEL 1

Dave's head felt hot. He had red spots on his face.

What do you think happened next?

| He ran around the block. | His mom took him to the doctor. | He went out to play. |

SAMPLE SHORT-SHORT STORY CARD FOR LEVEL 2

Betsy and Bert woke up early one Saturday morning. They were very excited because it had snowed all night. They put on their snowsuits and boots.

What do you think happened next?

Answer:

They went outside and built a snowman.

Predicting Outcomes: Short-Short Stories for Level 1

1. Nan and Lexi went to the city pool. It got cold and began rain. What do you think happened next?

> They went for a swim.
> They went home.
> They sat in the sun.

2. All the kids went to play on the slide. Scott got in line first. Five kids lined up behind him. What do you think happened next?

> Claire slid down the slide first.
> Scott slid down the slide first.
> Scott went to sleep.

3. Mike was playing ball. He did not see the bee. He stepped on it. What do you think happened next?

> Mike lost the ball.
> Mike had a slice of cake.
> The bee stung Mike.

4. Tim's bed was a mess. He piled lots of stuff on top of it. What do you think happened next?

> Tim jumped up and down.
> Tim's mom told him to clean off his bed.
> Tim played ball.

5. Dave and Brett were going fishing. They walked to the lake with their fishing rods. What do you think happened next?

> They played a game.
> They sat by the fire.
> They began to fish.

6. Kate picked up her jump rope. She went outside with it. What do you think happened next?

> She began to jump rope.
> She took a nap.
> She went shopping.

7. I looked around for my hairbrush. I saw it next to the sink. What do you think happened next?

> I took a bath in the tub.
> I brushed my teeth.
> I brushed my hair.

Comprehension

8. Mom put the dishes in the sink. She turned on the hot water. What do you think happened next?

> She washed her hair.
> She fixed a meal.
> She washed the dishes.

9. Becky bit her lip when she was eating an apple. It began to bleed. What do you think happened next?

> She went to bed.
> She put her skates on.
> She washed her lip.

10. I went to ride my bike. The tire was flat. What do you think happened next?

> I painted my bike red.
> Dad fixed the flat tire.
> I rode my bike.

Predicting Outcomes: Short-Short Stories for Level 2

1. Nate went out to feed his dog, Rover. Nate noticed that the dog was very dirty. He went back to the house and came back with a bucket, shampoo, and a towel. What do you think happened next?

2. Marsha and Amy were playing softball. Marsha was standing at home plate with a bat in her hand. Amy threw the ball from the pitcher's mound. What do you think happened next?

3. Marcy's alarm went off, and she got ready to go to school. She ate breakfast, brushed her teeth, and grabbed her backpack. While riding on the bus, Marcy remembered that she left her math homework on the kitchen table. What do you think happened next?

4. Five-year-old Steven was eating dinner with his family. While reaching for the salt, he tipped over his glass of milk. Milk spilled all over the table. What do you think happened next?

5. Lily went to the library and checked out a book about horses. Two weeks later it was time to return the book to the library. Lily looked all over the house, but she could not find the book. What do you think happened next?

6. Kristi and Luisa were best friends. They always seemed to be together. Kristi wanted to have a sleep-over. She invited Luisa to spend the night at her house. They ran to Luisa's house to ask her mother. What do you think happened next?

7. Patrick really wasn't a very good basketball player, but he loved to play the game. His coach knew how much Patrick loved the game, so he always gave him a chance. Late in one game, the score was tied. Suddenly, Patrick took a shot. What do you think happened next?

8. Andy has a little dog named Bubbles. Andy takes Bubbles for a walk in the morning and when he gets home from school. Bubbles is always on a leash. One day Andy and Bubbles came face to face with a much bigger dog that was not on a leash. What do you think happened next?

9. It was Jasmine's birthday. Her mother baked her a beautiful cake with eight candles. They lit the candles, and everyone sang "Happy Birthday." What do you think happened next?

10. When Mom got home from work, she was very tired. She told Kevin that she would take him out to dinner at a fast-food restaurant with a drive-through window. They drove to the restaurant, and Mom pulled up to the menu. What do you think happened next?

Extending the Skill:
Predicting Outcomes in Longer Stories

Materials Laminated story sheets (prepare on tagboard; see sample stories, pp. 159–161); strips of colored paper

Explain that while children are reading these longer stories, it will be as if they are operating their own video camera. You will be the director, and you may "stop the camera" at any point to ask children about what they think will happen next. This approach puts children right in the middle of the action. Prior knowledge and details from the stories help children make sensible predictions (realizing that there may be more than one good possibility).

Give children colored strips to place under the words as they read. This helps them track print, while also covering the following text so children can make their predictions without reading ahead.

While children are reading orally, call out "Stop the camera!" whenever you see the words "What do you think happened next?"

- For level 1, children are given three possible predictions. They should notice that two of them make sense, and either of these would be a good choice. They are to circle the event that they *think* will happen next. They then continue reading to see if their prediction is correct. This process continues until the story is completed. Be sure children understand that there is nothing wrong with a prediction that turns out to be incorrect. As long as it makes sense for the story, it is a good prediction and shows that they are understanding the story.

- For level 2, children make their own predictions, explaining them orally and supporting them with details from the story. Again, they should understand that any prediction that makes sense for the story is a good one, whether or not it turns out to be "correct."

After directed instruction in making predictions, provide uninterrupted time for struggling learners to reread for fluency.

Predicting Outcomes: Story for Level 1

Jade and Latoya went to the beach. It was a very hot day. The sand was hot on their feet. The two girls ran into the water.

What do you think happened next?

a. They ran out again because the water was very cold.

b. They stayed in the water and played with a ball.

c. They began to ride their bikes.

Jade and Latoya stayed in the water and played with a ball until their mom called them for lunch. They dried off and sat on a striped sheet to eat their lunch. When they were done, they went to play in the sand.

What do you think happened next?

a. They made pies out of sand and ate them.

b. Jade put sand all over Latoya's feet.

c. They made a big sand castle.

They made a big sand castle, but a wave washed it away. The girls laughed and ran back into the water to play.

Late in the day, it was time to go home. Jade and Latoya packed their things in their beach bags and walked to the car.

What do you think happened next?

  a. Before getting into the car, they brushed the sand off their feet.

  b. They ran back into the water.

  c. They put their beach bags into the trunk of the car.

Before getting into the car, they brushed the sand off their feet. Mom drove the car home. The day at the beach had been fun, but everyone was tired and happy to be home!

Predicting Outcomes: Story for Level 2

On Sunday the circus was coming to town. Carlos and David were very excited because their dad bought tickets. Carlos and David could hardly wait. Finally it was Sunday morning.

What do you think happened next?

Everyone piled into the car. As Dad drove, the boys could see the big red and white circus tent. They quickly found their seats in the first row. The boys had a great view of everything!

A clown in baggy pants rode a white pony into the ring. First he stood up on the pony's back. Then he tried to stand on his head while the pony trotted faster and faster.

What do you think happened next?

The clown flipped off the pony's back and landed on the ground. He held his head, jumped up and down, and cried very, very loudly, "BOO HOO HOO." But everyone just laughed. They knew he wasn't really hurt.

For the next act, two tigers ran into the ring. Their trainer held up a flaming hoop. He pointed at the tigers, cracked his whip, and cried, "Jump!"

What do you think happened next?

Finally, both brave tigers jumped through the flaming hoop. The trainer took a bow and led the tigers out of the tent.

Carlos and David watched many more great acts. When the circus was over, Dad drove them home. They can't wait for the circus to come back again!

MAIN IDEA

COMPREHENSION SKILL 6: Think about the relationships among the details of a reading passage and make a statement that describes the main idea.

The main idea of a story is a single statement that tells what the whole story is about. To identify the main idea, children sort through story details, think about the relationship among them, and make a statement that tells about them all.

Struggling learners sometimes don't understand the difference between a detail and a more general idea. Limited vocabularies can contribute to this problem. Oral and written classification activities are one way to develop children's vocabularies and also get them to understand the difference between details and general ideas.

Classifying works in two ways. You provide a list of related items, or details (such as *ring, necklace, earring, bracelet*), and children come up with the general category that describes them all (*jewelry*). You can also reverse the process, providing the main idea (such as *items to use when cleaning the house*) and asking children to list specific details that fit the category (*rags, bucket, mop, broom, vacuum,* and so on).

When the children have plenty of practice with classifying, extend the concept to simple stories in which they identify details, state the main idea, and explain how the details go along with or support the main idea.

Introducing the Skill: Classifying for Main Idea

Materials | Laminated cards with lists of related items (see suggestions below); also laminated cards giving only the "main idea" at the top; water-based markers

Provide cards with a list of related items for children to read orally. As they read, encourage active thinking. For example:

- Children read these words: *red, yellow, green, blue, orange, black, pink.*

- They think about what the words mean, form a mental picture, and realize that the words all name colors.

- Children then orally say and write the main idea of the list: *colors.*

Later you can reverse the technique, giving children a card that tells them the main idea rather than the list of details. They write related items (details) on the card under the main idea. Children reread their lists, checking to see that all the words support the main idea.

Main Idea: Lists for Classifying at Level 1

Clothing	Toys	Body Parts	Flying Things
pants	doll	chin	plane
jeans	truck	cheek	kite
dress	ball	hand	jet
socks	game	leg	bee
coat	blocks	toe	bird
belt	jump rope	nose	butterfly
jacket		lips	

Wheeled Things	Green Things	Hot Things	Pets
bus	grass	fire	cats
truck	plants	stove	dogs
bike	leaves	sun	fish
car	trees	grill	mice
train	peas	matches	hamsters
skates			snakes

Main Idea: Lists for Classifying at Level 2

Sports and Games	Kitchen Things	Parts of a House	United States Coins
hockey	stove	rooms	penny
baseball	oven	floors	nickel
soccer	dishwasher	roof	dime
basketball	refrigerator	walls	quarter
golf	can opener	door	half dollar
tennis	pots and pans	hallway	silver dollar
football		stairs	

Classroom Things	Things to Write With	Things to Read	Parts of the Earth
desks	pencil	books	mountains
chairs	pen	stories	deserts
chalkboard	marker	magazines	forests
teacher	chalk	newspapers	jungles
children	crayon	letters	grasslands
		comics	oceans

Musical Instruments	Things to Drink	Tall Things	Things in the Sky
piano	milk	trees	sun
organ	juice	telephone poles	moon
guitar	water		stars
flute	soda	basketball players	planets
violin	lemonade		clouds
trumpet	milkshake	skyscrapers	rainbow
saxophone		streetlights	
		giraffes	

Extending the Skill: Main Idea of a Story

Materials   Laminated story sheets (prepare on tagboard; see sample stories, pp. 164–166); water-based markers

Children orally read a story. After they read, ask questions to help them
think about the words and create mental images. When struggling learners
place themselves in the story, they can better visualize the details and how they

are related. Recognizing this relationship enables them to write the main idea of the story on the laminated sheet. Ask children to prove the main idea by listing details that support it.

Main Idea: Story for Level 1

My name is Tessa, and I just love to eat ice cream! I like any kind, as long as it is cold and sweet. It can be white, or brown, or pink, or green, or yellow. I like mint fudge ice cream and fresh peach ice cream.

I will eat it in a dish or in a cone. I would eat it out of the box if Mom would let me! I will eat ice cream with fruit, and I will eat it with cake.

Today I had a cone with three kinds of ice cream. Next time I think I will have an ice cream float, or maybe a shake. I think I could eat ice cream all day long, and all night, too.

What is the main idea of this story? _____

_____

Prove it! Write some details that go with or support the main idea.

_____

_____

_____

_____

Teacher-Directed Questions

1. Who is telling the story? (someone named Tessa)

2. What kind of ice cream does she like? (all kinds)

Comprehension

3. What are some of the flavors she likes? (mint fudge and fresh peach)

4. What are some ways she eats ice cream? (in a dish, in a cone, out of the box, in a float)

5. When does she like to eat ice cream? (all day long)

Main Idea: Story for Level 2

The old house looked frightening. The shutters on the windows were falling off, hanging by one old rusty nail. The front door banged against the wall, making a large hole with the doorknob.

The wind howled through the broken windows. Inside, cobwebs were scattered everywhere. A metal chain clanged on the stairs, making loud and scary noises. The steps were so old that they creaked every time someone stepped on them.

A moaning sound was heard coming from the room upstairs. It could have been a ghost. The house seemed to be haunted!

What is the main idea of this story? _____

_____

Prove it! Write the details that go with or support the main idea.

_____

_____

_____

Teacher-Directed Questions

1. What is the story about? (an old house)

2. What were the shutters doing? (falling off, hanging by one rusty nail)

3. What was the front door doing? (banging against the wall and making a hole in it)

4. What was the wind doing? (howling through the broken windows)

5. What was scattered everywhere inside? (cobwebs)

6. What made loud scary noises on the stairs? (a metal chain)

7. What happened every time someone stepped on the stairs? (They creaked.)

8. What was heard coming from the room upstairs? (moaning)

INFERENCE/DRAWING CONCLUSIONS

COMPREHENSION SKILL 7: From the details of a story, make inferences or draw sensible conclusions by "reading between the lines."

To make inferences and draw conclusions from something they are reading, children have to go beyond the text, or "read between the lines." Teaching the skill to struggling learners is a two-step process.

- First, we need to be sure children are getting the literal facts from the story. This may call for review and practice of Comprehension Skill 1, recalling details, with teacher-directed questions that lead them to identify who is in the story, what they are doing, and when and where this is happening.

- Then, once readers are confident about the literal details, they can learn how to infer nonliteral information. At this point, we teach children to be detectives, locating and using clues on the printed page to figure out something that is implied rather than written.

As with Comprehension Skill 5, predicting outcomes, it is critical that teachers establish prior knowledge about the subject matter of a story before reading begins. Children can't infer information or draw conclusions about something with which they are not familiar.

For example, children will have difficulty drawing conclusions about something that happens at a concert if they have never been to one, because even if they try to visualize the words, they cannot fully place themselves in the setting. But if we provide sufficient background information and help readers focus on the literal details of the story, they will be better equipped to draw conclusions that make sense.

Introducing the Skill:
Making Inferences from Short-Short Stories

Materials   Laminated activity cards with short-short stories and three possible conclusions to each (see suggestions, pp. 167–170); water-based markers

Children orally read each short-short story. Remind them to use active thinking as they read. Ask questions to help them focus on the literal details:

- Who is in the story?

- What are they doing?

- Where are they?

- When did that happen?

- Do you feel like you are in the story?

Children then read the three possible conclusions and circle the most sensible one. Have them orally identify and underline or circle the literal details in the story that support the conclusion they chose.

After teacher-directed instruction, children should reread the short passages for fluency.

Inference: Short-Short Stories for Level 1

1. Tom was so tired that he could not get out of bed. His face felt very hot. He had chills and hurt all over.

   What conclusion can you draw from this?
   a. Tom was happy.
   b. Tom was sick.
   c. Tom was funny.

2. Anna watched the pigs playing in the mud. She rode on a horse. She fed the sheep. She picked up eggs in the hen house.

What conclusion can you draw from this?

    a. Anna is at the mall.
    b. Anna is at the farm.
    c. Anna is at the beach.

3. Blake wanted to buy a new bike. He knew he must get a job. He began asking people if he could cut their grass.

What conclusion can you draw from this?

    a. Blake liked to cut grass.
    b. A bike is fun to ride.
    c. Blake needed cash to buy a bike.

4. When Seth was at the beach, he saw that his skin was getting red. He rubbed cream on his face and legs, but it was too late. His skin felt very hot.

What conclusion can you draw from this?

    a. Seth was on fire.
    b. Seth got a sunburn.
    c. Seth was bleeding.

5. Tim picked a red rose at home. On the way to school, he held the rose with great care. He smiled at his teacher when he gave her the rose.

What conclusion can you draw from this?

    a. Tim did not like his teacher.
    b. Tim did not do his homework.
    c. Tim liked his teacher.

6. Mr. Smith ran out of his house. He ran down the street to the bus stop. The bus drove past Mr. Smith as he ran.

What conclusion can you draw from this?

    a. The bus driver was mad at Mr. Smith.
    b. Mr. Smith was late for the bus.
    c. Mr. Smith liked to run.

Inference: Short-Short Stories for Level 2

1. Maria and Teresa got on the bus. They were wearing new shoes and new clothes. They had new backpacks filled with pencils and notebooks. Summer was over, and they were ready.

   What conclusion can you draw from this?

   a. Maria and Teresa were going on a trip.
   b. It is the first day of a new school year.
   c. Summer is finally here.

2. Casey, Bill, and Jake wanted to go to the movies. The only movie that was playing was a monster movie. Casey and Bill couldn't wait to go. Jake decided to stay home and play with his little sister instead of going to the movies.

   What conclusion can you draw from this?

   a. Bill didn't like monster movies.
   b. Jake didn't like his little sister.
   c. Jake didn't like monster movies.

3. Trisha gave her dog, Sparky, a large bone. Later, she saw Sparky sleeping in his bed. She couldn't find the bone she had given to him. When Trisha looked out the window, she saw a mound of fresh dirt near the fence.

   What conclusion can you draw from this?

   a. Trisha took the bone away from Sparky.
   b. Sparky buried the bone in the backyard.
   c. Sparky is a very playful dog.

4. Andrew went to the mailbox to get the mail. He found an envelope addressed to him. Inside was a birthday card from his grandmother. She also sent him some money. Andrew sat down and wrote his grandmother a thank-you note for his nice birthday present. He mailed his note to her the next day.

   What conclusion can you draw from this?

   a. Grandmother lived far away from Andrew.
   b. Andrew didn't like his grandmother.
   c. Grandmother lived in Andrew's house.

5. Mother gave the baby a bowl of cereal and a spoon. She turned around to get some milk when she heard a crashing sound. She turned back to see the bowl and the cereal on the floor. Mother got a rag and began to clean up the mess the baby had made.

   What conclusion can you draw from this?
   a. Mother spilled the milk on the floor.
   b. The baby liked her food.
   c. The baby pushed her bowl of cereal onto the floor.

6. One morning Sarah went to Mindy's house to play with her. Sarah rang the doorbell, but no one answered. She knocked very loudly on the door, but still no one came. Then Sarah remembered that Mindy has swimming lessons every morning.

   What conclusion can you draw from this?
   a. Mindy didn't want to play with Sarah.
   b. Mindy wasn't home.
   c. Sarah was at the wrong house.

Extending the Skill:
Making Inferences from Longer Stories

Materials   Laminated story sheets (prepare on tagboard; see sample stories, pp. 170–171); water-based markers

Children orally read a longer story. In response to questions, children circle the literal details that tell who is in the story, what they are doing, where they are, and when things happened. Then children choose the best conclusion from the three choices given.

Remind children to use active thinking, placing themselves in the setting of the story. They also need to be detectives, looking for clues to figure out what is happening that the words don't actually say.

Inference: Story for Level 1

Mike and Jan sat at their desks doing their math. Mrs. Wong walked around the room, helping the other kids with their work.

All at once, a bell sounded. Mrs. Wong told everyone to line up at the door. They left their work on the desks, walked down the hall, and went out the door. No one talked. Outside, Mrs. Wong made sure that all the kids were in the line. They lined up far away from the school.

After a long time, Mr. Chase said that they could go back into the classrooms. He told them that they did a good job.

What conclusion can you draw from this?

    a. The kids went outside to do their math.
    b. There was a fire drill.
    c. Mrs. Wong took her class outside to play.

Inference: Story for Level 2

One day while Marcus was watching television, he looked around his house. It was a mess! There were empty soda cans on all the tables. Newspapers were scattered all over the floor. Empty glass jars stood on the kitchen counters.

Marcus decided that he needed to get rid of the mess, but he didn't want to take it to the dump. Then he had an idea. He knew that some people were able to make old things useful again.

Marcus got into his car and drove to the store. He bought three large tubs, each one a different color. He labeled the red one "paper," the blue one "glass," and the yellow one "cans." He put the tubs in his shed and began to clean up around the house. He put all the empty cans in the tub marked "cans." He gathered up all the old newspapers and put them in the red tub. Finally, he picked up the glass jars and put them in the tub marked "glass."

When Marcus was done, his house looked beautiful! Everything was clean. From then on he always remembered to put the old newspapers, empty cans, and empty jars into the proper tubs.

In a few weeks, the three tubs were full. Marcus loaded them into the trunk of his car. He took them to the building where they take old newspapers, cans, and glass to make new things. Marcus was proud of how he helped to keep the earth clean.

What conclusion can you draw from this?

    a. Marcus went to college.
    b. Marcus decided to recycle.
    c. Marcus worked for the city.

CHARACTER TRAITS

COMPREHENSION SKILL 8: Identify the traits of a character, whether clearly stated in a reading passage or inferred from clues.

To identify character traits, we use words that describe people's personalities. For example, we might say that someone is *bossy, mean, kind, gentle, cheerful, loving, nosy,* or *shy*. The way characters act, the things they say, and what others say about them all help readers identify their individual traits.

Character traits can be important because they sometimes offer clues to help readers understand the events of a story and why they are happening. Actively thinking about character traits helps readers make sense of what they are reading and results in increased comprehension.

When character traits are clearly stated in a story, children have little difficulty identifying them. Often, however, the reader must infer character traits from clues in the story. This is more difficult for struggling readers. To help them, we ask questions that focus on characters' personalities. We help readers identify the clues that tell them what a character is like, and then link those clues to a general personality trait.

Introducing the Skill: Characters in Cartoon Stories

Materials   Laminated cartoon story cards, divided into sections with one sentence written at the top of each section (see illustrated example, p. 173, and suggested stories, pp. 173–175); water-based markers

Establish prior knowledge of the character traits you expect children to infer from what they read. For some struggling learners, this may involve vocabulary development.

Children then orally read a very short story. Ask them questions that focus on the main character:

- What did the character do?

- What did the character say?

- What did anyone else say about the character?

Children illustrate each sentence in the space below, using speech bubbles (as seen in cartoons) for dialogue. Once they have clearly visualized the story situation, they circle the appropriate character trait and write it on the line.

SAMPLE CARTOON STORY CARD

Jill was on the phone. Alex asked, "Who is calling you?"	Then Alex asked, "What are you talking about?"	Alex is _____.
		kind nosy helpful

Character Traits: Cartoon Stories for Level 1

1. Matt said to the old man, "Let me take your bag." Then he helped the man down the steps to his car. Matt is _____.

   shy   kind   bossy

2. Katy put the dishes away for her mother. She made tea for her dad when he was sick. Katy is _____.

   messy   mean   helpful

3. Fred always told everyone what to do. When the boys played games, Fred said, "We are all going to do things my way." Fred is _____.

   bossy   neat   sweet

4. Joey never wanted to meet anyone new. When someone he did not know came up, he would hide behind his mother. Joey is _____.

   nosy   loving   shy

5. Ali always puts her toys away. She never leaves things out because she does not want her room to look messy. Ali is _____.

    neat   rude   brave

6. Penny came home from school and dropped her books. When she changed clothes, she left her school clothes on the bed. Penny is _____.

    shy   messy   cheerful

Character Traits: Cartoon Stories for Level 2

1. Max was waiting for his turn with a video game. "Hurry up!" said Max. "I want to do it now. It should be my turn!" Max is _____.

    patient   quiet   impatient

2. Mother said, "Jenny likes to help me clean the house." Father said, "She always brings my slippers when I come home from work feeling tired." Jenny is _____.

    patient   thoughtful   annoying

3. Tony has a new dog. He brushes it and feeds it every day. He takes it for a walk in the morning before school. He makes sure the water dish is full. Tony is _____.

    sloppy   mean   responsible

4. Rodney saw a wallet on the sidewalk. He picked it up, looked inside, and saw a lot of money. Rodney looked at the address in the wallet. It was the house right in front of him! Rodney took the wallet back to the man who lost it. Rodney is _____.

    honest   gentle   nervous

5. "Why does it stay light longer in the summer?" asked Blake. "Who invented the telescope? Why are some stars brighter than others? Why does the moon have different shapes on different days?" His teacher said, "Blake, you sure ask a lot of questions." Blake is _____.

    brave   patient   curious

6. "Hi! You're new here, aren't you?" said Susan. "Would you like to play with me? We could play anything you like." Jesse said, "I'd love to. I just moved here and I don't know anyone." Susan is _____.

    shy   friendly   quiet

Extending the Skill: Characters in Longer Stories

Materials — Laminated story sheets (prepare on tagboard; see sample stories, pp. 175–178); strips of colored paper

Children orally read a longer story. They use highlighters, one color for each character, to mark the clues that suggest how each character acts or feels. Ask questions to encourage active thinking and to help readers place themselves in the story. After they have finished reading, help children look back at the highlighted clues and infer something about each character.

After directed instruction on character traits, give children uninterrupted time to reread the story for fluency.

Character Traits: Story for Level 1

Once upon a time there was an old yellow dog who lived near a brown cat. This old yellow dog was alone all the time. He did not laugh at all. He never had any fun. He had no one to play with him.

The brown cat saw how lonely the old yellow dog was. "One day I will make that old yellow dog laugh," said the brown cat. Then she began to think about ways to make an old yellow dog laugh.

The first day, the brown cat put on a funny hat to try to make the old yellow dog laugh. The old yellow dog just sat there. He said, "That's not funny."

The next day, the brown cat told some jokes. The old yellow dog did not laugh. He said, "That's not funny."

The third day, the brown cat did a silly dance with a bug on her nose. The old yellow dog just walked away without even a smile.

The brown cat gave up for a while. Then one sunny day, the brown cat said to the old yellow dog, "Come play with me. We can have some fun."

The old yellow dog said, "Who ever saw a dog and a cat playing together?" That was so funny, it made him laugh. And it felt so good to laugh, he went to play with the brown cat. After that, the old yellow dog smiled all the time because now he had a friend to play with!

Teacher-Directed Questions

1. Look at the first paragraph. What clues tell you how the old yellow dog acts or feels? Highlight them. (was alone all the time; did not laugh at all; never had any fun; had no one to play with him) From these clues, how would you describe the old yellow dog? (sad, lonely)

2. Look at the next few paragraphs. What clues tell you how the old yellow dog acts or feels while the cat is trying to make him laugh? Highlight them. (just sat there; said "That's not funny"; walked away without even a smile) From these clues, how would you describe the old yellow dog? (sad, hard to please, unfriendly)

3. In the story, what clues tell you how the brown cat acts or feels? Highlight them. ("Someday I will make the old yellow dog laugh"; put on a funny hat; told some jokes; did a silly dance with a bug on her nose; "Come play with me. We can have some fun.") From these clues, how would you describe the brown cat? (funny, silly, caring, friendly)

4. Look at the last paragraph. What clues tell you how the old yellow dog acts or feels? Highlight them. (made him laugh; felt so good to laugh; went to play; smiled all the time because he had a friend to play with) From these clues, how would you describe the old yellow dog at the end of the story? (happy, cheerful, friendly)

Character Traits: Story for Level 2

Everyone in school knew about Stanley. Stanley always acted like a clown. During math class he jumped up and yelled, "Watch me juggle!" Then he made the blocks tumble to the floor on purpose to make the class laugh. The teacher, Mrs. Chapman, glared at him, so Stanley sat down. In the middle of reading

class, Stanley interrupted again. He said, "Listen to this new joke I made up."
He told the joke, and everyone rolled on the floor laughing. His classmates
thought he was funny, but Mrs. Chapman didn't.

Mrs. Chapman said to him, "Stanley, stop trying to be so funny. Get your
work done. And let the other boys and girls work!" Stanley knew that Mrs.
Chapman was serious by the tone of her voice. He tried hard to behave for the
rest of the day.

The next day on the way to school, Stanley saw something shiny on the
ground. He bent down and picked up a bright gold ring. When Stanley rubbed
the ring, he felt a funny tremble in his body. And when the trembling stopped,
Stanley felt a little different. What could it be? He tucked the gold ring into his
pocket and went on to school.

All morning, Stanley sat quietly in his seat and completed all his work. Not
once did he interrupt Mrs. Chapman. The other kids began to whisper to each
other, "What's wrong with Stanley? Why is Stanley so quiet? When is Stanley
going to make us laugh?" Everyone was very confused by the new Stanley, even
Mrs. Chapman.

Finally Mrs. Chapman couldn't stand it any longer. She had to know what
was going on. She asked Stanley, "Why are you so good today? What is making
you behave so well?"

Stanley looked puzzled. "I don't know, Mrs. Chapman. On the way to
school, I found this shiny gold ring. When I rubbed it, I began to tremble.
Maybe this ring has magical powers that can turn a boy like me into a perfect
student." Everyone, including Mrs. Chapman, laughed!

Teacher-Directed Questions

1. Look at the first paragraph. What clues tell you how Stanley acts or feels? Highlight them. (always acted like a clown; jumped up and yelled, "Watch me juggle!"; made the blocks tumble to the floor to make the class laugh; interrupted; told a joke; classmates thought he was funny) From these clues, how would you describe Stanley? (silly, loud, rude)

2. Look at the first two paragraphs. What clues tell you how Mrs. Chapman acts or feels? Highlight them. (glared at Stanley; didn't think Stanley was funny; told Stanley "stop trying to be so funny," "Get your work done," and "Let the other boys and girls work"; knew Mrs. Chapman was serious by the tone of her voice) From these clues, how would you describe Mrs. Chapman? (strict, serious)

3. Look at the second paragraph. Is there any change in Stanley? Highlight any clue you find. (tried to behave for the rest of the day) What does this clue tell you about Stanley? (He's sorry for misbehaving; he wants to act better.)

4. Look at the third paragraph. What clues tell you how Stanley acts or feels? Highlight them. (saw something shiny on the ground; bent down and picked up a bright gold ring) From these clues, how would you describe the sort of person Stanley is? (He is curious.)

5. Look at the fourth paragraph. What clues tell you how Stanley acts or feels? Highlight them. (sat quietly in his seat and completed all his work; not once did he interrupt Mrs. Chapman; other kids whispered, "Why is Stanley so quiet?"; even Mrs. Chapman was confused about Stanley's behavior) From these clues, what type of boy does Stanley seem to be? (quiet, well-behaved, polite)

6. Look at the last paragraph. What clue tells you that maybe Mrs. Chapman isn't always strict and serious? Highlight it. (Everyone, including Mrs. Chapman, laughed.) What does this clue tell you about Mrs. Chapman? (She has a sense of humor.)

CAUSE AND EFFECT

COMPREHENSION SKILL 9: Recognize the relationship between events when one has caused another to happen.

When one event results in another event, we say there is a cause-and-effect relationship. The *cause* has to occur first; without the cause, the effect wouldn't happen. The cause tells *why* something happened, and the effect tells *what happened.*

Understanding these cause-and-effect relationships helps readers make sense of the sequence of events, resulting in increased comprehension. Children who recognize cause-and-effect relationships as they read are creating clear mental images of the events taking place in stories.

Some struggling learners have difficulty recognizing the logical sequence of cause and effect. When they read a sentence in which the effect is stated first, they tend to believe it took place first.

For example, they may read: *I jumped up to get a rag when I spilled my milk.* Because the effect, *I jumped up to get a rag,* is stated first, some children think it took place first and thus was the cause of *I spilled my milk.* Children fail to recognize the actual cause-and-effect relationship because they overlook the signal word *when.*

We need to encourage these children to actively think about and picture what the words mean, looking especially for signal words such as *so, because, when, since, therefore,* and *as a result.*

Limited prior knowledge about the subject of a story can interfere with children's recognition of cause-and-effect relationships. For example, to understand the relationship of someone *scratching because they have hives,* children need to know what hives are. When necessary, provide the background information children will need in order to understand what they are reading.

Introducing the Skill: Cause and Effect in Sentences

Materials   Laminated sentence strips (see suggested sentences, p. 180); water-based markers

This technique helps struggling readers to focus on the signal words that are a clue to cause-and-effect relationships, which in turn help them recognize the logical sequence.

- Children orally read sentences, circling any signal words that indicate the order of events.

- They underline and label the part of the sentence that tells why something happened (cause).

- They box and label the part of the sentence that tells what happened (effect).

Cause and Effect: Sentences for Level 1

1. When Bill tossed the ball to me, I grabbed it.

2. Kate cut her leg when she tripped and fell.

3. We dug a hole because we wanted to plant a tree.

4. Ali turned on the fan because she was very hot.

5. My mittens were soaked so I hung them up to dry.

6. The mouse ran into the hole when the cat chased it.

7. I jumped up to get a rag when I spilled my milk.

8. When Luke dropped the glass, it broke.

9. Mike needed to get glasses because he could not see very well.

10. The grass was very tall so Tami cut it.

Cause and Effect: Sentences for Level 2

1. The hiker stopped to drink from his canteen when he got thirsty.

2. The tire on Sandy's car went flat so she had to get it fixed.

3. The tire on Sandy's car went flat because she ran over a sharp nail.

4. I got a hammer and a nail so I could hang the picture on the wall.

5. Marcus stopped the car when he saw a line of ducks crossing the street.

6. Since the day was very hot, lots of people bought lemonade at our stand.

7. The creek flooded after we had six days of hard rain.

8. Sara's dog always runs and hides when he hears the water running for his bath.

9. The point on my pencil broke, so I sharpened it.

10. The barn burned down because it was struck by lightning.

Extending the Skill: Cause and Effect in Stories

| Materials | Laminated story sheets (prepare on tagboard; see sample stories, pp. 181–184); pencil and paper |

Identifying cause-and-effect relationships in stories can be difficult for struggling readers because stories have many details to sort through. After children orally read a story, ask questions that help them to recall and visualize the details (who, what, where, when).

For the questions that ask specifically about cause-and-effect relationships in the story, you might have children write the answers. Some questions state the effect (what happened) and children are asked to identify the cause (why); other questions state the cause (why) and children are asked to name the effect (what happened).

After teacher-directed instruction, give children the chance to reread the story for fluency and increased comprehension.

Cause and Effect: Story for Level 1

Last week, Emma went to a sheep and goat farm. She had never seen sheep or goats. She wanted to see what they did. The goats were brown and the sheep were white. They all ate grass. The farmer let Emma reach over the fence to pet the goats and the sheep.

One funny brown goat was digging a hole near the fence. He used his feet to dig. He made a big hole. The farmer wanted the goat to stop. If the goat dug under the fence, he could run away. So the farmer led the goat away from the hole and gave him some grain to eat. The goat didn't run back to the hole because he liked eating grain better than digging.

One tired white sheep only wanted to sleep in the shade under a tree. Then a bee came by and stung him on the nose! The bee sting woke up the tired sheep, who ran to the pond. When he stuck his nose into the cold pond, it felt a lot better. After a while, the sheep went back under the tree to sleep again.

Emma had a good time watching the funny goat and the tired sheep at the farm. Now she knew what sheep and goats did.

Teacher-Directed Questions for Recall of Detail

1. Who are the people in the story? (Emma and the farmer)

2. Who are the animals in the story? (goats and sheep)

3. Where is Emma? (on a farm)

4. What did Emma do at the fence? (reach over to pet the goats and sheep)

5. What did one brown goat do? (dug a big hole)

6. When did the goat stop digging? (after the farmer gave him some grain to eat)

7. What did the white sheep do? (slept in the shade)

8. What did the bee do to the sheep? (stung him on the nose)

9. When did the sheep go to the pond? (after he was stung)

10. When did the sheep go back to the tree? (after he stuck his nose in the cold pond)

Questions for Cause and Effect

1. When the goat dug in the dirt with his feet, what happened? (He made a big hole.)

2. Why did the farmer want the goat to stop digging? (because the goat could dig under the fence and run away)

3. Why didn't the goat run back to the hole after the farmer fed him? (because the goat liked eating better than digging)

4. When the bee stung the sheep on the nose, then what happened? (The sheep woke up and ran to the pond.)

5. When the sheep stuck his nose into the cold pond, then what happened? (His nose felt better.)

Cause and Effect: Story for Level 2

On Monday, Tori moved into her new house. When she looked around, she saw that she had a lot of work to do. But Tori didn't mind, because she was a hard worker.

First Tori went to the fireplace and looked up the chimney. She needed to clean the chimney because smoke from the fires had made it very dirty with black soot. To clean the chimney, Tori had to squeeze into a very tiny space. The black soot kept getting into her eyes and mouth, making it hard for her to breathe. She put on goggles and covered her mouth with a cloth to keep the soot away from her face. Tori was glad when that job was finished.

Next, Tori went out in the backyard. She got her ax so she could chop some wood to burn. Using the ax, she carefully split the wood into pieces. Then she neatly stacked the wood in the yard so it would be ready to burn in her clean fireplace.

After chopping and stacking the wood, Tori saw some broken boards in her fence. She gathered together a hammer, some nails, and new boards to fix the fence. She had just started to pound the nails when all of a sudden, one of the big boards slipped and fell on her foot. When she looked down, she saw a big gash in her ankle.

Tori rushed into the house to wash off the dirt and blood. Since she couldn't stop the bleeding, she knew she had to go to the hospital. A doctor put three stitches in her ankle to close up the gash and stop the bleeding.

What a long, hard day it had been. Tori will always remember the day she moved into her new house!

Teacher-Directed Questions for Recall of Detail

1. Who is in the story? (Tori)

2. Where does the story take place? (Tori's new house)

3. What did Tori see when she looked around her new house? (that she had a lot of work to do)

4. Where did Tori look first? (at the fireplace and up the chimney)

5. What made the chimney so dirty? (black soot)

6. When did Tori put on goggles and cover her mouth? (when she was cleaning the chimney)

7. When did Tori chop the wood? (after she had finished cleaning the chimney)

8. Where did Tori go to chop and stack wood? (into the backyard)

9. What did Tori use to chop the wood? (ax)

10. When did Tori see the broken boards on the fence? (after chopping and stacking the wood)

11. What did Tori gather to repair the fence? (hammer, nails, and new boards)

12. When did the board fall on her foot? (after she had started pounding the nails)

13. What did Tori do when she rushed into the house? (washed off the blood and dirt)

14. When did she go to the hospital? (after she realized she couldn't stop the bleeding)

15. What did a doctor do? (put three stitches in Tori's ankle)

Questions for Cause and Effect

1. Why didn't Tori mind having a lot of work to do in the new house? (because she was a hard worker)

2. What caused the chimney to be so dirty? (Smoke from fires left black soot.)

3. Why did Tori put goggles on and cover her mouth with a cloth? (to keep the black soot away from her face)

4. Why did Tori get her ax? (to chop some wood)

5. What caused Tori to gather a hammer, nails, and boards? (She had to fix a broken fence.)

6. When one of the big boards slipped and fell, then what happened? (It made a gash in Tori's ankle.)

7. Why did Tori rush into the house? (to wash off the dirt and blood)

8. What caused Tori to go to the hospital? (She couldn't stop the bleeding herself.)

9. Why did a doctor put three stitches in Tori's ankle? (to close up the gash and stop the bleeding)

BIBLIOGRAPHY

Cooper, J. David. *Preventing Reading Failure: Teaching the At-Risk Student.* California: The Education Center (n.d.).

Cunningham, Patricia M. *Phonics They Use: Words for Reading and Writing.* Reading, MA: Addison-Wesley, 1995.

Holt, John. *Learning All the Time.* Reading, MA: Addison-Wesley, 1989.

Howard, M. *Helping Your At-Risk Readers Be More Successful Readers.* Washington, DC: Institute for Educational Development, 1995.

Itzkoff, Seymour. *Children Learning to Read: A Guide for Parents and Teachers.* Westport, CT: Greenwood, 1996.

Linksman, Ricki. *Solving Your Child's Reading Problems.* New York: Fine Communications, 1998.

Sabin, Winston J. *Chapter I Teacher's Professional Guide to Reading Instruction.* Madison, WI: Center for the Study of Reading Program Administration, 1987.

Sykes, Charles J. *Dumbing Down Our Kids: Why American Children Feel Good About Themselves But Can't Read, Write, or Add.* New York: St. Martin's Press, 1995.

Teaching Reading: A Balanced, Comprehensive Approach to Teaching Reading in Prekindergarten Through Grade Three. Sacramento, CA: California Department of Education, 1996.